PIECES OF THE PAST

Department of the Environment for Northern Ireland

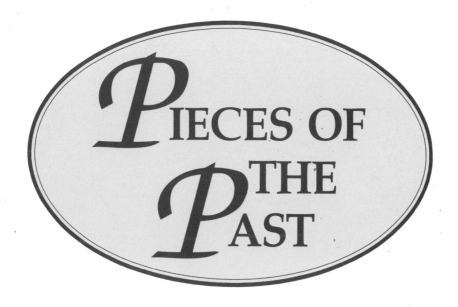

Archaeological Excavations by the Department of the
Environment for Northern Ireland
1970–1986

Edited by
Ann Hamlin and Chris Lynn

Belfast
Her Majesty's Stationery Office

ISBN 0 337 08216 2

CONTENTS

PREFACE

In the 19th century archaeological excavation was a pursuit for the 'nobility and gentry', as well as professional men like William Wakeman, art master at Portora Royal School. In the early years of this century one of its most active practitioners in east Ulster was the linen merchant, Henry Cairns Lawlor. A major change came in the early 1930s, when Estyn Evans and Oliver Davies, then young lecturers at Queen's University, started their important series of research excavations, concentrating especially on prehistoric stone tombs.

After the setting up of the Archaeological Survey* in 1950 there were, for the first time, professional archaeologists within government (at that time the Ministry of Finance). Dudley Waterman and Pat Collins combined field survey with a long series of masterly excavations, most of them promptly published in the *Ulster Journal of Archaeology*. These two founder-members of the Archaeological Survey set high standards which their younger colleagues and successors do their best to maintain. During the 1950s and early 1960s their excavation work was mainly in Co Down as part of the survey of that county, but as the 1960s progressed so the awareness of the destruction of archaeological sites grew and the need for 'rescue' excavation became clear. It was during these years, however, that the research excavation of Navan Fort was undertaken (1961–71), and our choice of a photograph by Pat Collins of Dudley Waterman's excavation at Navan for the frontispiece of this book is in tribute to their work. It provides a link with the period before the years covered by the book and serves as a foretaste of the Navan report, which will appear before long. As the staff of the Archaeological Survey increased in the 1970s the excavation effort grew and from 1970 onwards, the period covered by this book, work has been concentrated mainly on threatened sites.

Excavation in Northern Ireland is regulated by the Historic Monuments Act (NI) 1971, and since 1976 the Department of the Environment for Northern Ireland has been responsible for administering that Act through its Historic Monuments and Buildings Branch, of which the Archaeological Survey is part (see Appendix 2). The Department is the main initiator and funder of archaeological excavations, and of the 15 to 25 excavations licensed each year the majority are directed by the Department's archaeologists or by fee-paid staff on the Department's behalf. A list of all the excavations carried out by and for the Department during the period 1970 to 1986 will be found in Appendix 1.

The present book originated from the wish to make this work of archaeological excavation more widely known and to share some of the results of the past sixteen years. We hope that the excitement of discovery will emerge from these pages, and also that it will be clear that excavation is not only an absorbing activity but also a demanding one, both intellectually and physically.

The choice of 35 projects from several hundred was, of course, not an easy one. We have tried to include examples which illustrate the main types of activity, over the six counties of Northern Ireland, showing the very varied circumstances which can lead to an excavation and the results that can emerge – sometimes surprising, always interesting and in some way important in building up the picture of our past.

Many people have contributed to the book. Excavations by the late Dudley Waterman, Pat Collins (former Senior Inspector), the late Tom Delaney and Professor Peter Woodman are included. Other contributions cover work by the present staff of the Archaeological Survey and some fee-paid directors (indicated below by an asterisk). The identifying initials are as follows:

NFB – Nick Brannon
CF – Claire Foley
AH – Ann Hamlin
RJI – Richard Ivens*
CJL – Chris Lynn

---

* Since 1950 this term has been used for the group of professional archaeologists within government, but they are not concerned only with *survey*, as this book clearly shows.

JAMcD – Jacqueline McDowell*
MLS – Lesley Simpson*
KW – Ken Wiggins*
BBW – Brian Williams.

The line drawings are by Marion McLornan (MMcL) and the photographs are by staff of Historic Monuments and Buildings Branch, except where otherwise indicated in the captions.

I am grateful to all who have shared in the work, but especially to Chris Lynn, who originated and co-ordinated the project and saw it through to completion. His own major contribution to the excavation effort over the years covered by this book will be abundantly clear from its contents.

Ann Hamlin
Principal Inspector of Historic Monuments
Department of the Environment for
Northern Ireland

October 1987

Abbreviations

DOE(NI)	Department of the Environment for Northern Ireland.
HMBB	Historic Monuments and Buildings Branch, DOE(NI).
HMSO	Her Majesty's Stationery Office.
OS	Ordnance Survey, DOE(NI).
PRONI	Public Record Office of Northern Ireland, DOE(NI).
SMR	Northern Ireland Sites and Monuments Record, HMBB.
Ulster J Archaeol	*Ulster Journal of Archaeology.*

ILLUSTRATIONS

Front cover   Deer Park Farms, Co Antrim: surveying and recording in stone-lined entrance of 7th-century rath.
Back cover   Deer Park Farms, Co Antrim: oak door-jambs (felled AD 648) for use in a wicker house, during excavation in 1987.

Frontispiece   Navan Fort, Co Armagh: wall-slots of Late Bronze Age houses and post-pits of Iron Age multi-ring timber structure (1970).

A Warning

Searching for archaeological material by digging without an excavation licence, whether as a result of using a metal detector or in any other way, is strictly illegal under the Historic Monuments Act (NI) 1971 (*see Appendix 2*).

INTRODUCTION

People are interested in the past for many reasons, ranging from the purely academic study of ancient peoples to straightforward curiosity. We owe much to those who struggled to survive in ancient times and in conditions which today would be regarded as intolerable. The useful, but vague, concept of 'heritage' is sometimes applied to convey the continuity we have with earlier generations. If we want to learn more about antiquity than can be gleaned from accidental finds of ancient objects like pottery, weapons and stone implements, or from surface study of sites and monuments, then we must set out deliberately to uncover more of the evidence which is locked up in the ground. This means archaeological excavation which, though a specialist pursuit, is in fact very interesting and rewarding, something we hope this book will demonstrate.

For the period before history – before written records – the study of structures, burials, artifacts and domestic rubbish is the only means we have of finding out about how people lived in the past. Even for the 'historic' period (in Ireland from about AD 500 onwards) contemporary documents are sometimes very few and of little help in reconstructing the way of life. Study of material evidence, used in conjunction with the documentary sources, remains very important for finding out about many aspects of life in earlier times. The one method by which all the strands of evidence, including everyday objects, buildings, human remains, landscapes, environmental material and written records, can be brought together and related to one another in space and time is archaeological excavation.

This book is intended to demonstrate the great interest and wide range of information which is being recorded annually in excavations of Northern Ireland's archaeological sites and monuments. This is done by highlighting the particular interest of a selection of 35 recent archaeological excavations organized by Historic Monuments and Buildings Branch of the Department of the Environment (NI).

This introduction attempts to answer some of the main questions asked about excavations. Where are the sites? Why are some sites excavated and not others? How do we learn from excavation? How is an excavation carried out? What happens to the information? It sets the scene for the excavations which are described and illustrated chronologically, oldest first. Appendix 1 contains a list of all excavations carried out by the Department since 1970 including the types of site examined, the reasons for excavation and the areas in which excavations have taken place. Appendix 2 describes the law dealing with excavations and finds in Northern Ireland.

Where are the sites?

If we suppose that the countryside was usually occupied by the maximum number of people which it could support at any particular time it is easy to appreciate, given the long period of human settlement, that there is scarcely a field in Northern Ireland which does not contain some trace of ancient activity, from a single flint flake to the site of a dwelling and its associated features. To take the Early Christian period (AD 500–1200) as an example, the population of Ireland in those centuries has been estimated at about 200,000; a normal house may have sheltered five people and may have lasted on average twenty years. A simple calculation shows that we might expect there to be the sites of more than one million houses of this period scattered over the whole of Ireland! Even if only a small proportion of these, mostly wooden, houses has left traces which could be recognized in excavation, it is easy to see that the potential quantity of information which probably survives is enormous for the Early Christian period alone and this must be multiplied by the volume of traces of activity surviving from earlier and later periods.

Sites from which new evidence can be unlocked by excavation exist almost everywhere. We can recognize a proportion of them as upstanding monuments (mostly mapped by the Ordnance Survey) and others appear as distinctive cropmarks on aerial photographs. Other sites come to light accidentally, for example souterrains or cist-grave cemeteries (as at Straid, *p 12*) can be discovered in ploughing or road works. Some sites are discovered in the course of planned field-walking, involving the collection and mapping of scattered artifacts such as flints, as at Mount Sandel (*p 1*), or potsherds in a ploughed field, indicating a disturbed occupation site. Sites of later periods are sometimes known only from written sources, old maps and place-names, like the 'abbeys' of Massereene and Muckamore (*p 72*). Details of the locations and, where known, types and dimensions of all identified sites are lodged in the Sites and Monuments Record (SMR) of the Historic Monuments and Buildings Branch (DOE(NI)). The locations of about 13,000 archaeological sites are known in Northern Ireland at present (1987), but we must remember that there is a very large number of other sites about which we know nothing.

While excavations on these known sites can be very productive, archaeologists are concerned that not every type of past activity is adequately researched. Most of the excavations on Neolithic sites, for example, have taken place on burial monuments like Creggandevesky (*p 3*), but these are relatively few and presumably not everyone was entitled to burial in a special tomb or cairn. The information recovered from these monuments probably relates only to a minority of the population and then only to their beliefs about death and its attendant rites and not to their way of life. For nearly the whole of the 6000 years of Irish prehistory we know almost nothing about the location of the all-important settlement sites and we have to rely on chance discoveries of scatters of flint or pottery in ploughed fields or on recognition of hearths, gullies and artifact scatters in already damaged sites.

Which sites are excavated?
Archaeologists, particularly those working for a government department, do not generally (as many people imagine) systematically choose which sites to excavate and how much time to spend on the dig and on its report. Such a programmed process is usually described as *research excavation* and is designed to provide information to help in filling specific gaps in knowledge. A number of research excavations were carried out by the Department in the 1950s in conjunction with the archaeological survey of County Down

(HMSO 1966), and at Navan Fort and a number of megaliths in County Armagh in the 1960s. From long before the 1950s and 1960s, however, archaeologists have been aware of the enormous loss to the surviving, but unresearched, body of historic information brought about by the destruction of sites.

The attempt to investigate threatened sites and to recover as much information as possible before destruction is called *rescue excavation*. In this context the choice of sites is obviously determined by the threats, and the time available may be limited. The methods used are designed to get the maximum return of information in the time available, and if time is very short it may not be possible to do more than hurried *salvage excavation* as at Ballycraigy (*p 16*). On Downpatrick's Cathedral Hill, on the other hand, faced with the prospect of a graveyard extension it was possible to implement a rescue strategy over three years (*p 61*). Most of the rescue excavation done in Northern Ireland is carried out or sponsored by DOE(NI), which is charged by law with the protection of archaeological sites and monuments.

Information about threatened sites comes from a variety of sources, but especially the Department of Agriculture and the Department of the Environment's Planning Service. The regional offices of these and other public bodies have been circulated with a series of SMR maps showing all known sites in the area. If any planned development of which they are aware is seen to affect one of these sites HMBB is notified and an inspector assesses the archaeological implications and discusses with the owner possible ways of avoiding the monument. Destruction can often, but not *always*, be avoided and the recovery by excavation of information which would otherwise be lost for ever is seen as important, no matter what the type of site or the period involved. Rescue excavation does contribute towards *preservation* of the heritage, sometimes by demonstrating a site's interest and so bringing about its survival, as at Ballywee and Creggandevesky, or by preserving knowledge of the site in an archive and in a published report. Most of the excavations by DOE(NI) since 1970 have been carried out for rescue purposes (*see Appendix 1*). The Department considers that it is better to put resources into work which mitigates the loss of sites rather than to apply (inevitably) destructive research excavation to unthreatened monuments. But it is unhelpful to see a rigid distinction between the results of research and rescue work. Rescue excavation sometimes reveals hitherto unknown types of settlement or activity, and often uncovers remains of a quality and interest which could not have been foreseen in any research design as, dramatically, at Deer Park Farms (p 44).

Sites for rescue excavation are chosen on the basis of the quality and variety of the information likely to be revealed. Other factors are the time available and the location of the monument. For example, if two sites are threatened and only one can be dug, a relatively insignificant-looking rath in Fermanagh might be excavated, whereas an identical site in south Antrim – where excavations on raths have been plentiful – might not. Excavation is considered on urban sites for which there is clear evidence, from documentary references, old maps or observation of service trenches, that important archaeological deposits may well be present. *Trial excavation* on a small scale is sometimes done before a decision is made about whether or not to mount a larger rescue excavation.

Conservation excavations are usually small in scale and take place in conjunction with conservation or display works on State care sites as at St John's Point and Devenish (*pp 29 and 52*). It is sometimes necessary, for example, to underpin with a concrete foundation the wall of a masonry building which is leaning dangerously. The trench for the concrete must be excavated archaeologically to record details of the layers in such a crucial place. In other cases it may be necessary to excavate a trench for a water-pipe or drain or to expose the buried footings of a wall so that its line can be laid out on the surface. In the past some large excavations were carried out to expose the foundations of buried buildings for reconstruction and public display, but this type of work would rarely be considered today, though it would be needed to display Muckamore Priory to visitors (p 72).

How do we learn from excavation?

An underlying assumption in most of our interpretation of the past is that people in a particular area tended to do things – build houses, make pots and tools, bury the dead, design ornaments – in much the same way at a particular time. This combination of similar contemporary activities defines a 'cultural group'. In excavation, therefore, we try to see what objects, buildings, crafts, art styles, agricultural methods, foods and other things were in use together in one place (the excavated site) at one time. We try to find out what that time was so that the results of the excavation can be assessed in relation to results from other sites of similar dates.

Excavation may reveal a single phase of use, or a long period of activity divisible by distinct layers (stratification) into several phases, and these phases can also sometimes be distinguished by changes in the cultural material, such as pottery, settlement type or burial rite. It is, of course, rare to find all the evidence well preserved, and it is often the case that an excavation will be interesting mainly for one reason, like a well-preserved house, a good pottery sequence, or a wide range of animal bones, out of possibly a dozen categories for which data would be valuable. No one site contains all the answers, but by gradually building up information over many years from a variety of sites (like the four mounds described in this book, for example) archaeologists aim to develop as full an understanding of the way of life of people and the development of landscape at different times in the past as the material remains will allow.

While the archaeologist is interested in recognizing and comparing sites of the same date, it is of course important also to be able to organize the evidence in chronological order, to build up a sequence, and to tie it down whenever possible with firm dates. These can come from the already known date-ranges of certain types of objects, from documentary sources, from radiocarbon dates or from dendrochronology. In this way social and economic changes which took place over time can be suggested from changes in the artifacts, environmental samples like pollen, charcoal and seeds, and the changing architecture of the sites. This pattern must be constantly amended and updated as work progresses, and it builds up to form the 'story' we call prehistory, or archaeology's contribution to the understanding of later, documented, periods. Another type of variation is regional: people living in one area may not have lived in exactly the same way as a neighbouring group in an adjacent area, perhaps because of environmental differences between the regions, or because of a desire on the part of one or both groups to maintain and demonstrate different traditions.

How is an excavation carried out?

At a single-phase monument, like a cairn, the excavator is mainly concerned with recording the layout, method, sequence and materials of construction, and this can pose complex problems. Still more complex are the many archaeological sites, particularly in towns like Armagh, which contain traces of diverse human activities spanning hundreds of years. Recognizing, disentangling, recording and presenting this complex information in an orderly and efficient manner are major challenges for the excavator, and many techniques have been developed over the years to help in the task.

1 *Accuracy in recording: measuring distances, depths and angles with a theodolite.*

Stratification

An excavation team unravels in reverse order numerous 'contexts' (layers and individual features), each representing a different episode of activity on the site, deliberate or accidental, of long or short duration (*Figs 48 and 59*). The distinction between the soils of one context and another can be of great archaeological significance but is sometimes very slight in the ground and will be visible only to the experienced excavator. The basic principle is that a later layer will overlie one deposited earlier, and that where a dug feature (such as a post-pit or drain) intersects an earlier context the later feature will have intruded on the earlier one. Of course dug-out features such as ditches and post-holes are not found as open voids, as when originally made, but the distinct nature of their infillings helps us to identify and empty them and to work out their purpose.

Put at its simplest, archaeological excavation involves the recognition, recording and complete removal of distinct deposited materials, one at a time, in reverse order of deposition. The excavator hopes to be able to trace remains of every activity in the excavated area which involved depositing material on the ground or digging into it, always remembering, however, that some or all of the evidence could have been removed by later activity or weathering. The bases of built-up features like walls and banks often survive, but sometimes even these may have been thoroughly cleared away in the past leaving little trace, although their former presence can sometimes be deduced from other evidence like the plaster at Dungiven which survived after the wall was robbed away. While it is possible to recognize traces of some past events –

things people did on the site – it is not always easy to interpret these traces in terms of specific activities.

The Site Record

By accurately plotting the outlines, depths and profiles of every recognized feature and layer on a sequence of drawings, and by building up a written description of each of these separately-numbered 'contexts' the site archive accumulates (*Fig 1*). The archive is made up of everything that is carried away from the site: written records, drawings, photographs, notebooks, finds and samples. Ideally, the quality of this archive could be judged by testing its potential for making an imaginary reconstruction of the excavated site, with all its features and layers of the correct extent and thickness, using soils of similar types to the original and with every find and sample put back in its original place. Of course this is not done in practice, but the archive is used for the production of a detailed report in which the excavator tries to convey in a two-dimensional medium – writing, drawings and photographs – a complex of three-dimensional data. To this is added an interpretation, or a choice of interpretations, a judgement of what happened on the site which, in the excavator's view, best fits the objectively-recorded evidence of the soil. The excavator's *interpretation* can be revised in future, but the only evidence on which any re-interpretation can be based is in the excavation archive, and this is why excavation technique and recording must be of the highest possible standard.

Dating

The disentangling and recording of the layers and features establishes a relative chronology – the order in which layers accumulated and features were made. It does not allow close dating or assessment of how long a particular 'episode' lasted. A large pit, for example, could be dug and filled in a day or two while a very slight layer could have taken years to accumulate. One way of closer dating is by associated finds – objects characteristic of a particular period, most commonly pottery but sometimes coins – discovered in the layers and features. One danger is that finds may be 'derived', disturbed from an earlier context and incorporated into a later one, like the Neolithic stone axe in an 18th-century deposit at Downpatrick (*p 64*), but it is usually possible to attribute a layer to a period, like later Neolithic or Early Christian, or more closely, for example to the 9th or 10th century from a particular kind of bronze pin. Artifacts help in the dating of layers, and stratification in turn helps to refine our understanding of changing types of artifacts.

In recent decades several scientific methods have been developed to allow closer dating in terms of centuries or years. The measuring of residual radioactive carbon, ^{14}C, in excavated wood, charcoal or other organic material allows dating to within, on average, two centuries (*Fig 2*). Tree-ring dating – dendrochronology – can now tell us the actual calendar year in which a particular ring in a suitable sample of oak grew. If the outer rings of the tree survive, dendrochronology can establish the year of the tree's felling, and therefore arguably its first use on the site. The method is spectacularly illustrated in the chapter on the Dorsey (*p 21*). While dendrochronology is an extremely valuable dating method, it can only be applied when wood is preserved, usually at waterlogged sites, and these have only rarely been encountered in excavations over the last fifteen years, for example at Lough Eskragh and Deer Park Farms (*pp 17 and 44*).

The Finds

It may surprise the reader that so far we have mentioned 'finds' (artifacts) only in passing. Many people assume that archaeologists dig primarily to recover finds, for the interest of the objects themselves. Archaeological excavations, however, are hardly ever undertaken with the sole aim of finding artifacts and they are never carried out in such a way that the recovery of finds takes place independently of examining and recording the superimposed layers and the context (*see Appendix 2, p 96*). As objects are found, they are numbered, bagged and recorded routinely in the process of unravelling the stratification. Archaeologists use small tools like trowels because they are needed to peel off thin layers cleanly or to excavate small features, as well as to increase the chances of recovering small objects. Not every layer is likely to contain finds or delicate structural remains so the pace and method of excavation, particularly in rescue circumstances, have to be adjusted to the type and depth of the soil and the likely reason for its deposition. The discovery of an unusual object can certainly cause great excitement on an excavation and can add significantly to the potential for interpreting or dating the ancient activity on the site. Most of the objects, however, found in settlement sites were ordinary things, accidentally lost

2 Complex equipment in the Radiocarbon Dating Laboratory, Queen's University, Belfast.

or broken and thrown out with the domestic rubbish.

In the past people were less able than now to afford to lose or throw away tools or ornaments so that the absence of material indicating wealthy occupants, for example decorated metalwork, does not necessarily mean that the people were poor. Prized objects were carefully preserved, passed on or bartered in times of need, and some metal objects were undoubtedly re-cycled. The result is that excavated finds from rural occupation sites tend in general to reflect more mundane crafts: stone spindle-whorls, cooking pottery, knives, awls, hones, pins, querns, and so on. At some times in the past valuable objects were deliberately buried, for example bronze objects deposited in lakes and bogs for religious purposes, and in later times valuable metal objects including coins were sometimes hidden and never recovered, or simply lost as perhaps at Muckamore (*p 75*). These kinds of finds are of great interest but, not surprisingly, seldom turn up in the excavation of an occupation site.

By recovering a high proportion of the finds, some of which may seem insignificant individually, and noting their exact locations, we can interpret activity in various layers and places on the site, such as a metalworking area from slag, a flint-working area from waste cores and flakes, or a cooking area from cooking pottery. The distribution of finds may also suggest the likely intensity and duration of these activities and demonstrate how the activity pattern changed with time. In this analysis we tend to assume that objects were trampled into the ground where they broke or were lost, but sometimes it is possible to show that rubbish was collected and dumped periodically in a special place.

Conservation of artifacts and the reconstruction of pottery vessels is one of several tasks which must be carried out over a long period in a laboratory after the fieldwork phase of the excavation ends (*Fig 3*). It would not be right to remove ancient objects from a stable environment in the soil if they would suffer as a result. Metal, wood and leather objects are highly unstable and can disintegrate within hours if they are not carefully wrapped and supported on site until laboratory conservation can take place.

Other kinds of material, recorded in the same way as finds, are removed from the site for study in the important indoor phase of the excavation. These can be human and animal bones, soil samples for analysis and to be used for the extraction of pollen, charred seeds, insect remains and other materials, and charcoal for wood identification or radiocarbon dating. For practical reasons it is only possible to extract a fraction of the environmental evidence which any site contains, but study of samples can produce many kinds of information: for the human and animal population, for what was growing on or near the site, for the various activities which took place there, such as grain storage, stabling and butchery, and for the surrounding environment.

Publication

The process of excavation can certainly be very interesting for the participants, despite the often adverse conditions, but the fieldwork is unfulfilled if its results are not published. The work of excavation is best seen as a continuous process, from the taking of the decision to excavate to the publication of the completed report, although this seldom happens in practice. The compiling of the report can be as time-consuming as the excavation itself. Every layer and feature will have been described and illustrated in detail on the site, and this mass of data has to be reorganized and edited and publishable illustrations prepared. Similarly the finds must be catalogued and described, some will be drawn and their positions in the numbered sequence of contexts must be made clear. In addition specialist reports on human and animal bones, soils and environmental samples will need to be organized and incorporated into the report.

Archaeologists have to admit that excavation

3 Reconstructing large Neolithic bowl from 39 Scotch Street, Armagh, in HMBB Conservation Laboratory.

reports are seldom lively; they tend to be packed with facts and their significance may not always be immediately clear. Many DOE(NI) excavations have been published in recent issues of the *Ulster Journal of Archaeology* (*see Appendix 1*) and to see how a report is made up the reader is recommended to look at some of these. We hope this book will help to form a bridge between the work in the field and the final detailed reports.

Conserving the past

The aim of the Department of the Environment is to preserve for the future as many archaeological sites and monuments as possible. They are interesting places to visit; they are characteristic landmarks in our countryside and they are repositories of information, some of which can be unlocked in future excavations. There is no doubt that not only scholars but also increasing numbers of the public will continue to be interested in these sites. Archaeological monuments should therefore not be sacrificed for short-term economic gains, sometimes of trivial scale, nor should the resource be excavated extravagantly to satisfy present-day academic interests. Under the Historic Monuments Act (NI) 1971, all archaeological excavations have to be licensed by the Department (*Appendix 2*). The considerable costs, and the weighty requirement that the work be published in detail, ensure that research excavations are not numerous, and most of the Department's excavation effort between 1970 and 1986 has been directed towards threatened sites. Furtive, illegal and damaging excavations on archaeological sites, stimulated by the availability of metal-detectors used for treasure-hunting, do however pose an increasingly serious problem.

Archaeologists are acutely conscious that information of unique value for understanding the past cannot be replaced if an archaeological site is damaged or destroyed. We have a diminishing resource of sites and monuments which, unlike rare species in the natural environment, cannot regenerate or be re-introduced. The heritage of undisturbed archaeological sites can be likened to a library of irreplaceable ancient manuscripts which cannot be copied and which are incompletely indexed. These 'manuscripts' contain evidence (of variable but unknown interest) for activity at different places and times in the past. Only the cumbersome and inexact process of excavation enables us to open, read and interpret them. To continue the analogy, each time an archaeologist reads a page in this 'library' it is instantly destroyed, because excavation is a form of controlled destruction. Sometimes the owners of the manuscripts come into the library and deliberately or accidentally destroy a 'book'. In a proportion of cases, however, the archaeologists are alerted and allowed to read parts of the books before they are destroyed (through rescue excavation). Repair, maintenance and exhibition of other volumes owned by the library itself (State care sites) can cause damage to parts of the contents which must be read in advance (by conservation excavations). All of the manuscripts are suffering gradual decay, simply through the effects of time, weathering and infestation which we can do little to counteract. In these circumstances the Historic Monuments and Buildings Branch of DOE(NI), which is the appointed 'librarian', has a difficult and sometimes demoralizing task compared with the custodian of a more conventional library!

Although some monuments have been protected by law for over a century, only a small proportion of Northern Ireland's archaeological sites and monuments has statutory protection. Clearly, therefore, those sites which have survived to our own time have mostly survived because of the interest of their owners, past and present. In earlier years superstition may have helped to preserve monuments, but this has given way to appreciation of them as elements in the evolving landscape and a precious inheritance from the past. On the other hand, the availability of earth-moving machinery and of grant-aid for reclamation in recent years has resulted in increased rates of destruction in some areas. In addition, the continuing demand for stone, sand and gravel, the building of houses, factories and roads and the planting of forests all put pressure on the surviving monuments.

Against this background, the Historic Monuments and Buildings Branch of DOE(NI) puts much effort into informing the public, monitoring known sites and negotiating with site owners in order to preserve as much of the archaeological heritage as possible. It is always better, and usually cheaper, to preserve than to excavate, although this is not always possible in practice. This policy of preservation rather than excavation may seem odd in the light of the interesting results that have come from the excavations described in this book, and given the enthusiasm of archaeologists for excavation. But no matter how well the policy of conservation works there will always be a need for excavation. Our success rate in preserving threatened sites is improving, but the proportion of threats brought to notice before the sites are actually destroyed is also increasing because of more widespread monitoring, and so the demand for rescue excavation tends to remain constant. The future is obviously unknown, but it would certainly be rewarding if a greater share of the resource could be used for long-term research projects which would be likely to make the greatest contribution to knowledge and in which more people could be involved. It would also be desirable to devote more time to locating those important but largely unknown 'flat' sites of all periods, which could then be monitored and occasionally excavated as well as the upstanding monuments already known.

But no matter how it is applied in future, there is no doubt that excavation is one of the few processes which allow us to travel in time. We hope that the summaries of chosen excavations from the years 1970 to 1986 will convey something of the interest and excitement of exploration and discovery, and illustrate that the past is important to the people of Northern Ireland and well worth preserving.

What have we learned from these excavations?
In a book of this kind an emphasis on individual sites is inevitable, but just as field survey in the 1980s has moved away from a site-orientated approach to the study of landscape history, so the excavator's ultimate aim is to use the evidence from the individual site excavations – the pieces of the past of our title – to build up an ever fuller, more rounded picture of that past. So here we must ask how the DOE(NI)'s excavations from 1970 onwards have helped in filling out that picture.

The *Mount Sandel* excavation pushed man's earliest activity in Ireland back over 1000 years, well before 6000 BC. It uncovered an intensively used camp-site and much information about the economy of the Mesolithic dwellers beside the River Bann.

Evidence of Neolithic occupation remains elu-sive, but a quite unsuspected Neolithic ring-ditch was found in the middle of *Armagh* city. Knowledge of Neolithic stone graves has continued to grow, notably from the work on the court tomb at *Creggandevesky*, so excellently preserved under its covering layer of bog. This also serves as a sobering reminder of what must still survive in the countryside unrecognized under the blanketing upland peat. The court tomb at Tully, in an unexpected lowland location, remained undiscovered until 1970.

At *Altanagh* a superficially unpromising low mound was found to have been used for burial over a long period, from the Neolithic to the Late Bronze Age, and it contained an impressive range of prehistoric pottery. Bronze Age burials continue to be found regularly by chance, especially in quarrying and farm reclamation schemes. The rescue excavations at *Rathlin Island* and *Straid*, and others not featured in this book, help to fill out the distribution map of Bronze Age cemeteries, add significantly to our knowledge of pottery and human remains, and remind us of the settlements waiting to be found *somewhere* in the area of the burials. A fairly small rescue excavation demonstrated the artificial nature of the *King's Stables*, close to Navan Fort, allowing it to take its place among the 'ritual' shafts and pools found all over Late Bronze and Iron Age Europe, but not previously identified in Ireland. The work at *Kiltierney* would have been important for the iron La Tène fibula (brooch) alone, the first from an Irish excavation, but it also established the site as a distinctive form of Iron Age burial monument. When the chance arose to test the *Dorsey* enclosure, the results were dramatic: with the aid of dendrochronology, it was possible to date the large earthwork to exactly the same time as one of the major phases at Navan Fort, at about 100 BC.

The table in Appendix 1 shows that between 1970 and 1986 more excavations were done on Early Christian period sites than sites of any other period. Excavations on secular settlement sites have tended to confirm the variety which written sources suggest. *Ballywee* was not an 'ordinary' rath, though its rectangular house and souterrains would not be out of place in a rath. The wooden souterrian found in the rath at *Coolcran* reminds us that distribution maps of stone souterrains may not accurately reflect the distribution of all types of underground refuges. Field survey has demonstrated that extensive remains of settlements and fields of many periods survive in upland areas, and the *Ballyutoag* excavation established the Early Christian period date of one settlement enclosure, quite different in type from the familiar raths and cashels. The results of a series of rescue excavations on Early Christian period mounds over the last sixteen years are nothing short of spectacular. At *Big Glebe* a mound exactly like an Anglo-Norman castle mound was built in the Early Christian period, a major piece of engineering requiring substantial resources. Other mounds have been shown to have grown in stages: three main phases at *Gransha*, four at *Rathmullan* and five at *Deer Park Farms*. One rewarding feature of these sites is that structures are often unusually well preserved from having been buried deep under subsequent occupation surfaces. Were these mounds occupied by people of special importance, lofty in rank as well as physically elevated? The evidence from these excavations allows this and other important questions to be debated.

The study of the early church has been advanced significantly by recent excavations. In *Armagh* the earliest burials go back at least to the 6th century, only a century after St Patrick's time, and the unsuspected large hilltop cemetery at *Dunmisk* also seems to be very early. Here there was evidence for a wooden structure, perhaps a church, and the work at *St John's Point* suggested that the surviving stone church had been preceded by a wooden structure. A policy of examining archaeologically any disturbance of the ground near a known early church site has had interesting results. *Movilla* and *Tullylish* are two of a number of examples where evidence for Early Christian activity has been found outside a visible site nucleus, including at Tullylish two substantial enclosure ditches. Recent work at *Downpatrick* has indicated an Early Christian period date for the ditch around the hilltop rather than the prehistoric date earlier suggested. At Armagh, Downpatrick, Movilla, Tullylish and *Devenish* important structural remains have been found from the medieval period as well as from the earlier phases of use of the sites. This recent work on ecclesiastical sites has also stimulated discussion of the size, nature and organization of the settlements and sharpened

our anticipation of the threats to the buried elements of these sites.

The excavation at *Rathmullan* showed that the Anglo-Normans had chosen an already raised settlement mound as the base for a motte, and four medieval phases were uncovered. The close dating made possible by coin finds has brought about some rethinking of traditional dating of pottery in the 13th century. There was not as much castle excavation in Northern Ireland in the 1970–86 period as during the preceding two decades, but the long programme at *Greencastle* continued. The excellent stratification in the rock-cut ditch was important, both for understanding the castle's history and for dating the finds. The small excavation at *Tildarg* was done as part of the programme of upland fieldwork, to test an unusual rectangular enclosure. The dating of the house to the medieval period was important, to students of building history as well as archaeologists, as very few rural houses of the Middle Ages have been excavated in Ireland. At *Muckamore* and *Massereene* the position of the two 'lost' religious houses was established and elements of the plans were uncovered, leading at Muckamore to the preservation of the whole site.

Urban archaeology was in its infancy in Ireland when the long series of excavations in *Carrickfergus* began in the early 1970s, and the more recent work in *Coleraine* and *Belfast* has given us the first glimpses of the buried history in those towns. In these two cases the policy of concentrating work on documented sites was pursued to good effect, for example on the 'citadel' at Coleraine and on Belfast Castle. In our final example, at *Dungiven*, many strands of enquiry converge: the priory site had long been in State care and some excavation had been done in and around the church, but documentary and pictorial sources focused attention on the priory as the site of a late medieval castle and a Plantation period house and bawn. Excavation was done to test the theory, and the house was found, as abandoned in the late 17th century. The re-use of monastic houses for secular occupation has been less studied in Ireland than in Britain, and the Dungiven story suggests that more research on this subject could be fruitful.

1. IRELAND'S EARLIEST HOUSES

MOUNT SANDEL
Co Londonderry

C 854307

Scheduled

In the early 1970s housing was expanding quickly south of Coleraine, along the east bank of the River Bann. It was approaching the large earthwork known as Mountsandel Fort, and archaeologists knew that over the past hundred years collectors had found distinctive Mesolithic flint material in this area. When, therefore, a field immediately north-east of the fort and zoned for housing was ploughed in 1972, Peter Woodman of the Ulster Museum walked the ploughed land looking for flints. He found enough to justify organizing some exploratory excavation in 1973. Expectations were not particularly high because the area had been ploughed for a very long time, but in four seasons of work, 1973, 1974, 1976 and 1977, Peter Woodman uncovered the earliest settlement yet found in Ireland. The expansion of 20th-century housing led to the discovery of houses more than 8000 years old.

Traces of the houses survived because they were in a slight hollow and had therefore been protected from plough damage (*Fig 4*). There had been at least four rebuildings and there were four large, sunken hearths. The wall lines showed as arcs of post-holes, the posts angled inwards, and the excavator suggested that they had been saplings or boughs bent and tied together at the top, covered with skins and perhaps turves (*Fig 5*). There were less clear traces of where other structures had stood, and evidence for the zoning of different activities: an 'industrial area' with much flint waste material, areas with deep pits for storage or rubbish, and groups of post-holes suggesting racks.

4   Excavation of the Mesolithic houses in progress.

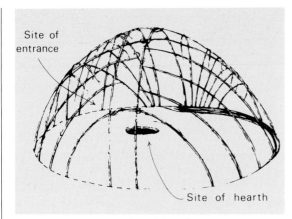

Site of entrance

Site of hearth

5 *Possible reconstruction of hut framework* (drawing *R Carson*).

The main finds were flints – tens of thousands of pieces, both implements and waste. Most common were microliths, tiny worked flints which often must have formed parts of a composite tool, like the barbs of harpoon (*Fig 6*), but there were also axes for heavier work. Only burnt bone survived, but the remains included pig, fish (especially salmon, trout and eel), birds and a dog. Plant remains were also rare in the acid soil, but hazelnut shells were plentiful.

The evidence suggested that the Mount Sandel settlement had housed a small group for at least the winter months, perhaps for longer. They had hunted, fished, caught birds, gathered wild plant foods and used stored resources, like hazelnuts. For the rest of the year the group must have travelled, exploiting the countryside elsewhere, but returning for many years to this settlement beside the Bann. Radiocarbon dating indicates use between 7000 and 6500 BC, in the Early Mesolithic period. A second settlement of this very early period has been excavated more recently at Lough Boora in Co Offaly, and perhaps others await discovery.

The Mount Sandel results are fascinating in themselves, but the work also illustrates several

6 *Were microliths used like this?*

important general points. It is always valuable to consider earlier investigations: the discoveries of amateurs during a century of flint collecting pointed to the importance of the Mount Sandel area. Field-walking after ploughing can provide clues to concentrations of material and indicate where excavation might be worth while. Finally, there are many important archaeological sites which do not show any surface features. Some will be found by accident, and some will be identified by careful 'detective work', like Mount Sandel, but many others must still remain to be found.

AH

Collins A E P, 'Excavations at Mount Sandel, lower site', *Ulster J Archaeol* 46 (1983), 1–22.
Woodman, P C, *Excavations at Mount Sandel 1973–77* (Northern Ireland Archaeological Monographs: no 2, HMSO, 1985).

CREGGANDEVESKY COURT TOMB
Co Tyrone

H 643750

State care

In 1979 this slight elevation, on a high glacial esker ridge overlooking Lough Mallon, was only just recognizable as an archaeological site: a long low cairn, largely covered with peat, with the tips of a few big stones showing. Identification as a court tomb seemed likely, but so little was visible that it was quite possible that the monument was badly destroyed. When a land reclamation scheme was proposed, involving the removal of the cairn, an excavation was arranged (*Fig 7*). It continued over four seasons, from 1979 to 1982, with spectacular results and a happy outcome.

The first task was to expose the surface of the cairn by removing the covering peat and heather. Next, all the loose, collapsed and slipped stones were taken away to reveal the original outline of the monument. This was time-consuming but

rewarding, as it emerged that, far from being badly ruined, the cairn had been well protected by its own collapse and by the growth of peat.

The cairn was found to be trapezoidal in plan, 18 m long and 13 m wide at the front (east) end,

8 The court during excavation. The green tip of the capstone was just visible before excavation.

7 The excavation in context.

where a semicircular open court gave access to the burial gallery (*Fig 8*). It decreased in width and height from front to back. The cairn's sides were revetted with drystone-walling, surviving to a maximum height of 1.75 m, skilfully constructed to resist the thrust of the loose cairn material behind. The amount of fallen stone suggested that these retaining walls could have stood 2 to 3 m high when first built. The burial gallery within the cairn was divided into three chambers by projecting jamb stones. The chambers decreased in size and height from front to back, echoing the cairn's trapezoidal ground plan and wedge-shaped elevation.

The Creggandevesky excavation greatly increased our understanding of the architecture of megalithic tombs: the state of survival was so good that structural details which have usually disappeared remained to be studied and recorded. When stones were not tall enough, for example, drystone-walling was used to fill the gaps. The large lintel over the entrance seems to have been carefully chosen for its symmetry and to form the highest point of the tomb. On the outside it is supported by large blocks, but inside drystone-walling was used to add height to the burial gallery. A detail which seemed to bridge the gap in time between the builders and the excavators was a small chocking stone inserted between the lintel and the western portal stone. This was clearly to level up the lintel which, without it, would have leaned uncomfortably to one side. The considerable difficulties of manoeuvring such large stones into precise positions above head height were probably overcome by the use of ramps, ropes and levers.

The burial gallery had been roofed with corbelled slabs. These had partly collapsed into the chambers, together with much cairn material. When this collapse was excavated it became clear how the corbelling had worked. The lower corbels were still in position, large granite blocks, firmly anchored into the cairn at an angle of about 45°. Lying on the burial deposits was a quantity of thin sandstone slabs, some lying vertically as though they had fallen from a height. The suggested interpretation is that these were used to bridge the gaps which could not be spanned by the granite corbels.

9   The 'old pile of stones' excavated, secured and displayed.

The first chamber would have been about 2 m high inside the entrance, and there was a marked decrease in height from here to the end of the burial gallery.

As the name indicates, court tombs are thought to have been built for burial and associated rituals, and the unravelling of the evidence for burial at Creggandevesky was particularly important. Cremated human bone was found in several places, especially around the entrance and in the front of the burial gallery, but perhaps because of the acid soil no unburnt bone was found. It is quite possible, however, that there were originally some inhumations (unburnt burials): for example in the second chamber there was no bone but three flint arrowheads, a flint awl and a flint scraper were found there. Could these be grave-goods deposited with a now vanished burial? Other flint implements were found elsewhere in the gallery, including a javelin-head, arrowheads, a scraper and knives, also a necklace of 112 stone beads and the very fragmentary remains of seven round-bottomed, shouldered Neolithic bowls.

Analysis of the cremated bone by an anatomist showed that there were remains of five males, seven females, one adolescent, and eight other individuals. The bone was very fragmentary and may have been deliberately crushed after cremation. There was a large area of scattered charcoal centrally placed in the court, but no associated scorching of the ground. This is unlikely to be the site of a fire but must represent the scraped-up remains from a fire. Radiocarbon dating suggests a date in the middle of the 4th millennium BC (5500 before present), so it is reasonable to conclude that this was the burial place of one of the earliest farming communities in the area.

The excavation started in 1979 because the cairn was threatened with destruction, but it aroused such great local interest and revealed such an impressive monument that the farmer agreed to leave the site which is now secure and in State care (*Fig 9*). The work has shown what valuable archaeological information can lie below superficially unimpressive remains, a lesson which must encourage caution in evaluating similarly obscured sites during field survey. It has also demonstrated what care and skill were devoted to this major Neolithic engineering project 5½ thousand years ago. These 'rude stone monuments', so-called by 19th-century antiquarians, were not so 'rude' after all!

CF

3. RECOGNITION, RECORD AND REBURIAL

TULLY COURT TOMB
Co Fermanagh

H 124561

In 1970 a Fermanagh farmer was levelling an irregular raised area, overgrown with thorns, on a south-facing slope, 1 km from the south-west shore of Lower Lough Erne. The work was halted when some large stones were uncovered, apparently part of an ancient structure, and inspection of the site by an archaeologist from HMBB confirmed the existence of a previously unrecorded megalithic tomb.

The site was totally excavated in 1976 by a DOE team directed by D M Waterman because it appeared that the cairn would have to be removed. Before excavation the tops of three upright stones in line were visible above the modern surface, and these turned out to be the eastern side-stones of a burial gallery. Eleven displaced slabs lay strewn over the surface of the low mound which stood barely 45 cm above the surrounding field. The 1970 work had caused only slight damage, but most of the cairn and the upright stones of its western half had been removed in some earlier clearance operation, creating the lop-sided picture seen in Fig 10.

The monument was cleared of topsoil and modern accumulations to expose the top of the surviving cairn, its revetment walls, chamber, side-stones and jambs. Where no stonework remained, particularly on the western side, sockets

10 *Remains of court tomb laid bare.*

11 *Excavation plan.*

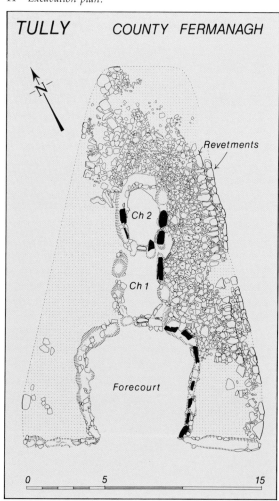

TULLY COUNTY FERMANAGH

Revetments

Ch 2

Ch 1

Forecourt

0   5   15

for the missing uprights were uncovered (as at Ballinran, *p 7*) and the complete plan was revealed (*Fig 11*).

This slight hump in the field turned out to be the remains of a Neolithic court tomb. The wedge-shaped cairn was 23.5 m long. A forecourt 7 m wide, entered over a sill, led to a burial gallery with two large chambers, separated by a sill between a pair of jamb stones. The sides of both chambers were formed of three large upright slabs.

The stones retaining the forecourt and the front of the cairn were set in continuous bedding trenches up to 30 cm deep. The forecourt had been disturbed, but enough was left of a compact layer of stone slabs, carefully placed on the natural surface, to suggest that the court had been blocked deliberately, perhaps when the tomb was considered full? The floor of the first chamber had been scorched red by burning, and a deposit of burnt soil and charcoal on this floor contained the cremated remains of two children, one under five, the other between six and ten years old. There were also two small sherds of Neolithic pottery. On the floor of the second chamber was a deposit of grey clay containing the burnt remains of a young adult male, a single fragment of a second individual, a stone bead and a flint flake.

The cairn was retained round its sides with a crude wall of large sandstone boulders, surviving only on the east side. Outside this functional revetment, 40 to 90 cm away, was a free-standing, neatly-built 'false revetment' and the space

6

between was filled with rubble. The outer revetment added nothing to the stability of the cairn and must have been added for the sake of appearance.

With its two-chambered gallery, the Tully tomb belongs to the most widespread type of court tomb in north-west Ireland. On the other hand, its orientation is unusual, aligned 27° west of south rather than east, and it is set at a lower altitude than is usual for court tombs in Fermanagh: most are in land over 150 m while Tully lies at 75 m above sea-level.

Though this tomb was badly damaged, excavation succeeded in revealing and recording the complete plan and many interesting features of its construction. When the work was finished the remains of the monument were covered with a low mound of soil to protect the intact stonework and to allow farm machinery to pass over it. All traces of this previously unrecognized but important Neolithic tomb could so easily have been destroyed in a few minutes with a bulldozer. It is thanks to the keen observation and the interest of the owner that the tomb was investigated and its remains have been preserved.

CJL

Waterman, D M, 'The excavation of a court cairn at Tully, County Fermanagh', *Ulster J Archaeol* 41 (1978), 3–14.

4. X MARKS THE SPOT

BALLINRAN
Co Down

J 194154

In the 1830s and 1850s the six inch Ordnance Survey map of Co Down marked a 'Giants Grave' at Killowen, just south of the road between Rostrevor and Kilkeel and close to the shore of Carlingford Lough. By the early years of this century, however, the maps showed only the 'site of' the grave, with the characteristic cross which marks a vanished site on an Ordnance Survey map (*Fig 12*).

In 1976 a road-widening scheme was planned which would remove this 'site' and an excavation was organized by A E P Collins. Although no traces survived above ground, excavation showed that the holes in which the stones forming the grave had once stood were clearly visible in the subsoil. Indeed it was possible to trace the plan of an unusually large court tomb, even though no stones survived except a single stump (*Fig 13*). The characteristic forecourt, facing north towards the Mourne Mountains, opened into the burial gallery which had been divided into five or six segments. A small quantity of cremated human bone was found in some of the stone sockets, but finds were sparse. The contrast with Creggandevesky (*p 3*) could hardly be greater: there an almost intact

12 *The site on the OS six inch map.*

tomb still enveloped in its cairn, here a 'megalith' without stones.

This excavation showed that the Ordnance Survey map-makers had been admirably accurate in placing the cross to mark the site of the destroyed monument. It also showed in a very impressive way how an apparently lost site can be 'resurrected' by careful excavation. It was a brief resurrection, because the road-work soon followed, but the plan of the 5000-year-old tomb was recovered and now forms part of the ever-growing

body of information about this important type of
Neolithic monument.

AH

Collins, A E P, 'A court grave at Ballinran, County
Down', *Ulster J Archaeol* 39 (1976), 8–12.

13   *Plan of the stone sockets.*

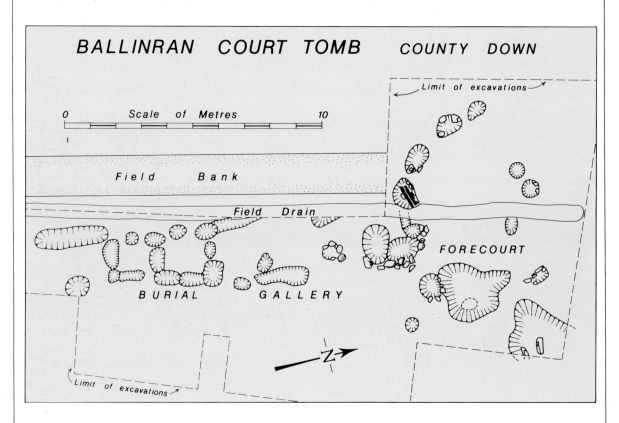

5. ARMAGH IN 3000 BC

39–41 SCOTCH STREET
Armagh City

H 876451

Generations of Armagh citizens and tradespeople
had no idea that only a few centimetres under the
floors and pavements of Scotch Street lay the
remains of a prehistoric enclosure dating back
more than 4000 years.

A series of small excavations has taken place
in Armagh since the mid 1970s, mainly in advance
of redevelopment arising from bomb damage in
the narrow streets of the city's business centre. The
archaeological interest of the Scotch Street area has
been well known since the mid 19th century, when
William Reeves pointed out that it crosses the site
of *Na Ferta*, a cemetery and sacred place tradi-
tionally dating back to the time of St Patrick (*p 58*)
It was in the hope of recovering some information
about this ancient and enigmatic Early Christian
site that work began in the winter of 1979 on a large
area previously occupied by shops.

The demolition of the shops and bulldozing of the site had caused much disturbance to the underlying soil, but Early Christian and medieval period graves and other contexts, cut into the surface of subsoil, were soon recognized. It also became clear that a fainter, more regular, large feature underlay all the Early Christian deposits. As this outline was carefully traced it turned out to be a filled-in ditch (*Figs 14 and 15*), roughly circular in plan and up to 12 m across internally. Its filling was a mixture of silt, redeposited subsoil and occasional patches of dirty soil and charcoal. There was no sign of an accompanying bank or palisade. The site of an entrance to the enclosure was marked by a gap in the ditch on the south-east, 80 cm wide, and the ditch was widest and deepest on either side of this gap.

The ditch had a V-shaped profile, steep on the inner edge but more gradual and difficult to trace on the outer. It was 1.1 m deep on average and the same in width. No other features were found which seemed likely to be of the same age as the

14 *Neolithic ditch during excavation.*

15 *Plan of Neolithic ditch (later features in broken outline).*

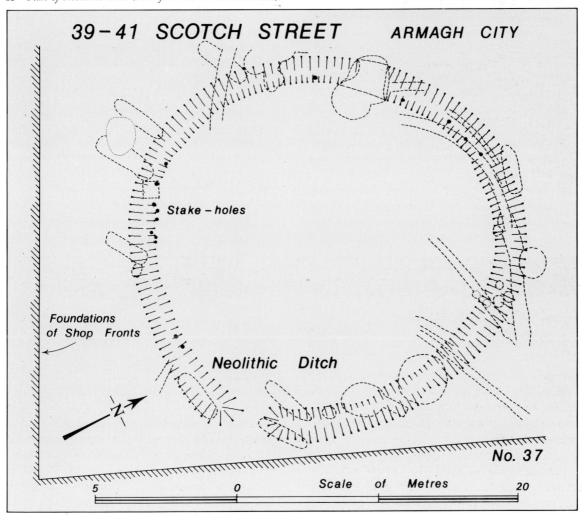

9

ditch. No other prehistoric features were recognized apart perhaps from some stake-holes which lay in an arc roughly following the curve of the ditch, but it was clear that the stakes had been inserted after the ditch had completely filled up. The lack of other prehistoric features may result from the extensive but generally shallow recent disturbance of the surrounding surface.

The surprisingly early date of the ditch was demonstrated by the discovery of hundreds of small pieces of Neolithic pottery, representing several dozen different vessels, found mixed up in the infilling of the ditch. Seven of the vessels were decorated with impressed patterns, while others were plain bowls or cooking pots. After long and painstaking study it has proved possible to reassemble large portions of two decorated vessels (*Figs 3 and 16*). From the surface of the ditch fill came two sherds of 'Carrowkeel Ware', a type of Neolithic pottery normally associated with the people who built passage tombs. Some of the fragments of broad-rimmed decorated vessels occurred in small scatters of dozens of joining sherds, associated with spreads of charcoal. Samples from two of these charcoal layers were dated using radiocarbon analysis and this indicated that the ditch was probably dug within a few centuries on either side of 2800 BC.

The interpretation of the ditch remains a puzzle. It is possible that it was filled deliberately over a relatively short period in a series of separate episodes. But observation of the gritty subsoil after rain showers during this winter excavation suggested that the ditch would have silted up fairly quickly, even if left untouched. The size and layout of the ditch point to a ritual interpretation, at least by analogy with similar sites elsewhere, like ring-

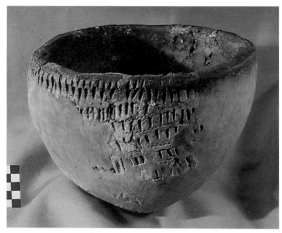

16   *Reassembled Neolithic vessel.*

ditches in England, but it must be admitted that at present there is little comparative evidence from Ireland. On the other hand the character of the infilling, which included flint objects and animal teeth, could indicate normal domestic activity, but there were no traces of a building in the enclosure, nor any of the small pits and hearths usually associated with a dwelling area. It is possible that a similar Neolithic feature will one day be found elsewhere, with clearer evidence for its function, but in the mean time this Armagh site remains significant for the large Neolithic pottery group and for its demonstration of activity here more than 3000 years before St Patrick's time.

There was no evidence that the space inside the ditch was covered by a mound and the ring-ditch can only have been visible, if at all, as a slightly sunken ring when the area was next used in the Early Christian period (*p 57*).

CJL

ALTANAGH
Co Tyrone

H 623693
Scheduled

Long-hidden evidence for prehistoric burial ritual lay on the summit of 'Crockgallows', a steep gravelly hill about 3 km south of the village of Carrickmore. Who could have known that a cemetery of the Neolithic and Bronze Ages lay below the unimpressive mound which crowned the hilltop? Initial excavations by local school teachers revealed the potential of the site and as the mound was threatened with levelling, three seasons of further work were arranged, from 1979 to 1981.

Activity seems to have begun in about 2500 BC when burials of cremated bones were placed in shallow pits, accompanied by plain and decorated Neolithic pottery, flint arrowheads, and simple personal ornaments. Later a stone structure, probably a court tomb, was built as a more elaborate burial place. Finds of cremated bones, elegant Neolithic bowls and flint arrowheads were recovered, similar to the finds from the pit burials, and a radiocarbon date indicated that the tomb may have been used for burials around 1800 BC.

The practice of burial on the hilltop continued in the succeeding Bronze Age. Cremations placed in pits and cists (stone-lined pits) were accompanied by beautifully decorated food vessels. Another change in the burial practice occurred in about 1300 BC, when cremated bones were placed

18   The Bronze Age pottery on display.

in large urns. Three cordoned urns were found, one upright (*Fig 17*) and two inverted over the cremated bone, in circular pits. They were packed around with carbonized twigs of hazel and willow, presumably debris from the cremation pyre, and fragments of pig and cow bones may have been remnants of a funeral feast. Two parallel slots in the ground near these burials and of similar date may have been part of an associated mortuary structure. As the intact urns were uncovered it was clear that they looked much as they must have done when buried over 3000 years ago (*Fig 18*).

After the cordoned urn burials the hilltop cemetery fell into disuse. Following a long period of abandonment, perhaps more than 1500 years, the summit was modified to form a rath, a type of monument normally interpreted as an enclosed farmstead of the Early Christian period. Little evidence survived here of domestic structures, but simple bowl furnaces with associated slag showed that ironworking had been an important activity on the site around AD 500. Iron objects found near the furnaces included ferrules, goads, a penannular brooch and a sword. This was a rare opportunity to excavate and study such objects, not because they were necessarily scarce in the Early Christian period, but because iron objects do not readily survive.

Following the end of Early Christian period activity little else can be traced from archaeological

17   Cordoned urn during excavation.

evidence on the hilltop, but ploughmarks show that the land was worked in subsequent generations, and a cache of carbonized oats was dated by radiocarbon to the 17th century AD. Despite the place-name, 'Crockgallows', and the local tradition that this was a place of public execution, no trace was found of the gallows!

BBW

Williams, B B, 'Excavations at Altanagh, County Tyrone', *Ulster J Archaeol* 49 (1986), 33–88.

7. SALVAGING BURIALS WITH A BULLDOZER

STRAID   C 596058
Co Londonderry

Once or twice a year HMBB receives a report from the police or forensic scientists that human remains, probably ancient, have been accidentally discovered. Such a call to the Archaeological Survey, early in February 1985, led to the rapid investigation of seven Bronze Age burials near Claudy in Co Londonderry.

The driver of a bulldozer, levelling a gravel ridge in a land improvement scheme, had dislodged the large capstone of a long stone cist, revealing inside a well-preserved human skeleton and an intact, highly-decorated pottery vessel. This was not a previously-known archaeological site, but it seemed likely that the cist was part of a Bronze Age cemetery, and that other cists awaited discovery. The ground surface had been thoroughly disturbed, however, and was partly snow-covered, and large stones or soil discolorations which might have indicated the presence of other graves could not be seen. Given these circumstances, and the unavoidable total destruction of the site, the most suitable technique for finding more cists was to continue machine clearance, but under archaeological supervision. So, with the co-operation of the landowner and the bulldozer driver, the gravel was gradually scraped away while the archaeologist and interested local people looked on.

Three more cists were found. The second, a small, cube-shaped example, was damaged by the machine, but yielded the fragmented remains of a large urn and cremated bones. The two other cists were recovered intact, their locations revealed when the bulldozer blade scraped across the massive stone slabs which covered them. Stronger members of the onlookers joined forces to lever the slabs carefully off the cists, exposing the skeletons and their accompanying pots to the sky for the first time in 3500 years.

The first cist, which had brought the site to notice and stimulated the investigation, contained the remains of a robust man, 188 cm (6 ft 2 ins) tall, who had died aged about 22 years. The anatomist who reported on the remains found that the skeleton had a well-developed right shoulder, suggesting that this prehistoric man might have been a carpenter or sawyer. Next to his skull lay a tripartite bowl, highly decorated with comb-tooth impressions and zig-zag lines, and with a star-shaped ornament on the underside (*Fig 19*).

The second cist contained the cremated remains of an adult male and a 3 to 4 year-old child, sex unknown. The large urn found with them, a tall conical vessel, had probably been inverted over the burned bones and ashes. The third cist contained the remains of three individuals. Most prominent was the skeleton of a man, 180 cm (5 ft 11 ins) tall, who had died in his mid 30s (*Fig 20*). Next to his skull was a small decorated bowl, but under his left arm and his right foot (and therefore placed in the cist before his burial) were the cremated remains of two women. Anatomical

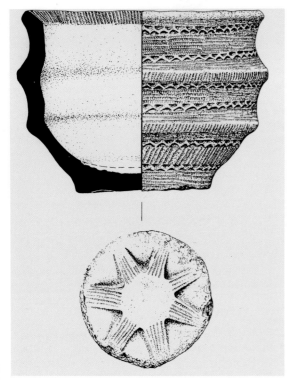

19 Tripartite bowl from first cist (drawing D Warner).

20 Skeleton of arthritic man in third cist.

study showed that the man had suffered from osteoarthritis, probably so severely that he could not have had an active, physical life. The fourth cist contained the skeleton of a 168 cm (5 ft 6 ins) tall man, who died in his late 20s, and again a decorated pottery bowl had been placed next to his head at the time of burial.

In no case was the cause of death clear. Certainly none of the skeletal remains showed marks consistent with severe wounds. 'Natural causes' or 'cause of death unknown' must therefore be the verdict on the seven individuals found here.

The discoveries raise numerous questions which archaeologists can discuss, weighing interpretation of the physical evidence against the unknowns of Bronze Age burial practice. Was the posture of the corpse of religious significance, or was the size of the cist, and hence the posture of the corpse, a practical consequence of the size of the stones available to build it? What was the significance of inhumation as opposed to cremation – ethnic or social status, for example? Was cremation used as a way of preserving remains

until a cist was available? Were the ornate pots which accompanied the burials made specifically for them? Did they contain food or drink, long since decayed? Does this imply belief in an afterlife?

The seven burials in this small cemetery provide a glimpse of the physical remains and perception of death of a Bronze Age community who lived in the Claudy area around 1600 BC. The settlement site in which these people lived, and which might preserve traces of buildings, remains undiscovered. Neither it nor the cemetery showed any above-ground remains which the archaeologist can at present recognize, and indeed most Bronze Age cists are not intentionally revealed by archaeological excavation but come to light accidentally, as in this case. Only the lessons learned from accumulated evidence will enable prehistorians to pinpoint such sites in advance of their destruction and answer some of the questions raised by this chilly salvage excavation.

NFB

CHURCH BAY, RATHLIN ISLAND
Co Antrim

D 149508

Church Bay is the site of the main landing place on Rathlin Island, off the north coast of Co Antrim (*Fig 21*). An area of Church Bay, immediately south of an isolated standing stone, has long been known to be of archaeological significance. In 1784 a Dr W Hamilton noted that 'a number of small tumuli were lately opened' and that 'the chief himself lay in a stone coffin and beside him an earthen vessel . . . a large fibula was found in one of the tumuli'. This 'fibula' is the splendid silver penannular brooch now known as the 'Demesne, Rathlin, brooch' which is in the National Museum of Ireland in Dublin. Tumuli and stone-lined graves in the same location were described by Mrs Gage in 1851, by the Rev J O'Laverty in 1887 and by H I Law in 1961. From the scattered earlier accounts Richard Warner of the Ulster Museum had recently concluded that this small area contained an Early Bronze Age cemetery of stone cists and that there was also settlement, activity or burial hereabouts in the Early Christian period and perhaps, more specifically, evidence for Viking contact with the island.

Within this well-documented area was a pasture field immediately south-east of the main settlement of Rathlin, behind the post office. This was to be quarried for gravel in the late autumn of 1983, as part of a plan to construct an enlarged harbour. When HMBB was alerted, small-scale gravel digging had already started; at least one burial had been exposed and others perhaps removed (*Fig 21*). Responding to this news, HMBB

21   Church Bay with quarry site on left of houses.

dispatched a small team to the island (the first time an official group of this nature had been on Rathlin), with a brief to observe the quarrying as it progressed, to record accurately any features that might be exposed, and to recover any finds.

It was not long before the excavators saw for themselves one of Hamilton's 'stone coffins', as the first of seven cist burials was revealed. This was a compact rectangular box, little more than 1 m in length, composed of several slender limestone slabs placed neatly on end, with a single large capstone on top. Inside lay the well-preserved bones of a young woman in her early 20s, the skeleton resting on its right side in a crouched position (*Fig 22*). Cist graves of this type are well known in the Irish Bronze Age and generally date from around 1600 BC. However, it was a novelty on Rathlin for such a tangible relic of antiquity to be drawn and photographed with meticulous attention to detail, and the islanders took a keen interest in the work.

22   Crouched burial in cist.

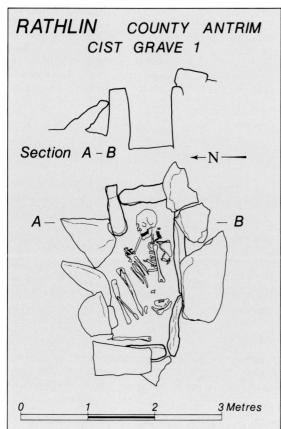

A second cist housed the remains of five individuals together with an intact food vessel, a type of Bronze Age pot commonly associated with burials. These may have contained some form of nourishment for sustenance on the journey to the next world. The straight-sided pot was decorated with twisted cord impressions. This cist was surrounded by a small ring-ditch, 6 m in diameter. Grave 3 contained the bones of a child aged about six, which, appropriately, were accompanied by a pygmy cup, a sort of diminutive food vessel, standing only 9 cm high. The cup was decorated with incised lines in a geometric pattern.

The final burials, numbers 6 and 7, lay side by side in the quarry field, and were very fine examples of their type. Thick limestone slabs were used as uprights and each cist was set in a pit, lined with limestone and floored with small, irregular, limestone slabs. A crouched skeleton on its right side, a female in her late teens, was found in grave 6. The occupant of grave 7, a male skeleton of about 25 years, lay on his back with arms across the chest and knees drawn up under the chin. The graves contained similar pots: sophisticated vase-like vessels decorated with zig-zag impressions formed by a small bone comb.

The salvage excavations confirmed the long-standing belief that Church Bay was the site of a prehistoric cemetery, further remains of which may survive undisturbed outside the quarried area. It would obviously have been preferable to excavate the entire field scientifically, in the hope of finding evidence for the growth and layout of the whole cemetery, and for traces of subsequent occupation, rather than relying on the quarry machines halting when they hit cists. Nevertheless, the number of graves recorded and the artifacts recovered made the venture more than worthwhile. Early Christian period finds also indicate settlement on the site at that time and could provide a context for Viking Age burials. We must hope that some of these await discovery elsewhere in the vicinity. Perhaps a future excavation on Rathlin will enlarge on the picture as we now understand it, and provide answers to the questions raised by this limited salvage investigation.

KW

Warner, R, 'The re-provenancing of two important penannular brooches of the Viking period', *Ulster J Archaeol* 36 & 37 (1973–4), 58–70.

BALLYCRAIGY
Co Antrim

D 384039

In April 1985 an archaeology graduate walking across a housing development site in Larne noticed an arc of fourteen boulders protruding through the bulldozed surface. Realizing that these might indicate the presence of some kind of monument, he contacted HMBB archaeologists. With the co-operation of the developers a salvage excavation was rapidly organized, revealing the previously unknown and unsuspected remains of a Bronze Age ritual site (*Fig 23*).

The developers' machines had effectively stripped the site down to subsoil clay or bedrock. All that survived was a circular ditch, of approximately 12 m external diameter, which had been cut down into the subsoil and so escaped destruction. Filling the ditch were two layers of clay. The lower layer was devoid of 'finds' and probably resulted from erosion, while the upper layer contained fragments of burnt bone and sherds of Bronze Age pottery, so-called 'flat-rimmed ware'. Lying on the surface of this clay layer, and exactly paralleling the line of the infilled ditch, was the arc of boulders which had revealed the presence of the site to the keen eye of the finder.

The excavation indicated a sequence of events: the digging of the ditch, its filling and the laying out of a line of boulders. Working through this sequence the archaeologist can create a chain of deduction which, though not susceptible of absolute proof, can at least offer a plausible reconstruction of the site's history and provide one explanation for the archaeological traces which survived.

23   *Archaeology and construction work side by side.*

At a practical level, the original digging of the ditch must have produced an upcast of clay and stone which may have been removed from the site or used to create an earthwork. The most likely earthworks in this context would be either some form of concentric bank or an inner mound, creating the kind of monument we would call a barrow. But no earthwork had been noted on the site or on Ordnance Survey maps, and it must either have been very slight or have been destroyed at an unknown period, before the early 19th century.

The lower infilling layer, being a clean clay and free of finds, can be interpreted as deriving from natural erosion of the ditch edges which took place when there was little or no rubbish, indicating little human domestic activity, in the area. The upper layer, however, was of a more mixed consistency and contained burnt bones and pottery fragments of Bronze Age date. The bone was too fragmentary for firm identification as animal or human.

Alternative interpretations would be that the bones are animal (food debris) or human (cremations), while the pottery had either a domestic or a ritual function. If the 'finds' are of ritual origin, formerly cremations contained within pottery vessels, then their fragmentary state within the clay layer shows that the burials were broken up and dispersed, perhaps when their religious value had been forgotten. It is also possible that the layer containing the finds was itself entirely redeposited, that is, derived from elsewhere.

It is, therefore, possible to build up a picture of an open ditch encircling an earthen mound which contained cremation burials, the whole then being levelled, with the dispersal of the mound and the burials into the ditch.

The survival of the arc of stones was fortuitous and traces of stone sockets elsewhere suggested that a full circle of stones had once occupied the site. That the stones so accurately paralleled the line of the infilled ditch rules out coincidence, and it is possible that the line of both ditch and stones was determined from a separate, unknown, point or area, for example an inner bank or mound now destroyed. Alternatively, the similarity of alignments may reflect a virtual contemporaneity of events. The postulated earthwork destruction and infilling of the ditch were perhaps the first stage in the creation of a new monument, one occupying the same space but incorporating a stone perimeter rather than a ditch. A change in ritual practice, or possibly religious belief, is indicated.

The discovery of burials *in situ* or other archaeological traces which would have confirmed the finds as ritual, rather than domestic, debris would clearly have been valuable. Irrespective of the interpretative chain of thought developed above, the physical evidence of the previously unknown site remains on record. Further investigation of similar sites may in the future clarify our understanding of the Ballycraigy ring-ditch.

NFB

10. ARCHAEOLOGY ALMOST UNDER WATER

LOUGH ESKRAGH
Co Tyrone

C 770620

Archaeological sites were hidden from view and preserved for thousands of years under the waters of Lough Eskragh, a small lake a few kilometres west of Dungannon (*Fig 24*). Several areas of wooden piling, a crannog, two dug-out boats, and many interesting objects were revealed in 1953 when the water-level in the lough was considerably lowered by the drawing off of supplies by the Moygashel Textile Mills. The sites were again exposed, twenty years later, in similar circumstances, but the water-level dropped so low that the sandy lake bed dried out, causing the destruction of one site and threatening another. Excavation was therefore undertaken in November and December 1973, in poor winter weather. The work was quite dangerous on the soft peaty mud of the

24 *Lough Eskragh.*

25 *One-piece alder bucket (27.2 cm high)*
(drawing S McKnight).

lake bed, which had the consistency of thick por-
ridge! Routeways were constructed over the mud
using wooden duck-boards, and journeys off the
main duck-board routes were made using tea-
chest lids, stepping from one lid to the next, lifting
one at each step.

In prehistoric times Lough Eskragh was
smaller than at present and was surrounded by
pine forest. Remnants of this forest survived as
tree stumps below the water as the lake increased
in area. Flint arrowheads and points found along
the old shore-line provide evidence for wildfowl-
ing and fishing around the lough.

Two dug-out boats, each more than 7.4 m
(24 ft) long, had been found in 1953 close to a
crannog, which was set a little distance out from
the old shore-line. Finds on this brushwood and
timber man-made island in 1973 included two
intact pottery vessels, a wooden bucket carved
from a solid alder trunk (*Fig 25*), a jet bracelet, a
polished stone axe and six saddle querns, which
may have been used for grinding grain. It looked
as if the occupants had left the crannog expecting
to return, but had failed to do so. An oak plank
found lying on the surface gave a radiocarbon date
of 700 BC.

Nearby, close to the old shore-line, a long
group of almost 600 birch and ash piles was found,
driven into the soft peaty mud of the lake bed. Piles
from different parts of the group were shown to be
contemporary, as the pointed ends had been trim-
med with an axe with a recognizable notch in its
cutting edge. One of the piles gave a radiocarbon
date of 500 BC. Fifteen saddle querns were found
lying amongst the timbers.

Further north along the shore a lakeside platform of brushwood and timber, similar in construction to the crannog, was dated from one of its
timbers to 1100 BC. Burnt daub found around the
perimeter of the platform was interpreted as the
remains of an enclosing fence destroyed by fire.
The surface was littered with broken clay moulds
used in the manufacture of bronze swords and
axes, together with clay crucibles and a stone anvil,
and the site is best interpreted as a Late Bronze Age
smithy. A similar lakeside settlement on the north-
east shore, with two small mounds encircled by
double or triple rings of piles and abundant burnt
daub, had been recorded in 1953, but was destroyed by fissuring of the dried lake bed in 1973.
All that remained was a broken saddle quern and
two wooden piles, one of which provided a radiocarbon date of 400 BC. On the western shore a
linear group of wooden piles was observed for the
first time in 1973. Fragments of saddle querns
among the timbers indicated a prehistoric date for
the structure, but before it could be fully recorded
and sampled the water-level suddenly rose and
covered the sites again.

Who knows? Will twenty, 200 or 2000 years
elapse before an archaeologist has an opportunity
to see these sites again? But in 1973 the three areas
of wooden piles, together with the crannog and

brushwood platform, gave us a rare glimpse of Late Bronze Age lakeside settlement between 1100 and 400 BC.

BBW

Collins, A E P and Seaby, W A, 'Structures and small finds discovered at Lough Eskragh, Co Tyrone', *Ulster J Archaeol* 23 (1960), 25–37.

Williams, B B, 'Excavations at Lough Eskragh, County Tyrone', *Ulster J Archaeol* 41 (1978), 37–48.

11. MAN-MADE RITUAL POOL?

THE KING'S STABLES, TRAY
Co Armagh

H 838455

State care

This unique and puzzling earthwork, now covered in small trees, lies about 1 km west of Navan Fort (*Fig 26*). Its unusual name must come from one of the legendary kings of Ulster believed to have lived at nearby Navan Fort. It is one of the few sites where even the hardened archaeologist is struck by a strange feeling of the unknown. The impression is heightened by the site's secluded location: in pasture, near a small marsh between glacial hills, with the central mound of Navan Fort just visible in the distance. The hill immediately to the west is crowned by the slight remains of 'Haughey's Fort', probably a Bronze or Iron Age enclosure.

At first sight the monument looks like a small, nondescript rath with a low, overgrown, spread-out bank, absent on the west side. But there is no external ditch (usual with raths) and the interior of the site, within the bank, measuring some 30 m across, is 2 m lower than the surrounding land

26 *The King's Stables.*

surface. The peculiarity of the site does not end there. The surface of the interior is treacherous, floating, sphagnum peat which quakes ominously if anyone foolishly ventures on to its edge (*Fig 27*). The monument was, even before excavation, clearly an artificial pool of great antiquity and the surrounding bank was evidently material upcast from construction of the large circular basin. The peculiar aura of the monument is emphasized by the local tradition that the pool is inhabited by a 'dragon' which has emerged from time to time to discourage interference.

In 1975 the owner proposed to drain the pool because of the danger it posed to his stock, but he agreed to suspend work to allow time for a trial excavation. Fortunately that summer was very dry and with continuous pumping it was possible to excavate rapidly two long, 2 m-wide trenches, running on a north-west to south-east diameter into the edges of the pool and through the bank on the south-east. These demonstrated that the pond was indeed artificial, with a flat bottom on bedrock more than 2 m below the present boggy surface. The original earthen sides of the pool were steep and regular but it had filled up with layers of organic mud, peat and, at the edges, clay washed down from the bank.

Only about 5 per cent of the silted-up pool was excavated and its centre could not be examined at all for reasons of safety, but this small excavation produced important finds and evidence of the past environment. The artificial pool had clearly been continuously water-filled from the start, as many chopped twigs, which would not otherwise have been preserved, lay on the very bottom. Mixed up

27 *The treacherous interior.*

in the primary silt at the edges were eighteen small pieces of clay moulds (refuse from the manufacture of bronze swords), two sherds of coarse pottery of Late Bronze Age or Early Iron Age type and two objects of bone, one a spatula made from antler, the other a small broken scoop. While these finds pointed to a date for the construction of the monument in the Late Bronze Age (*c* 1000–500 BC) (and this was corroborated by three radiocarbon dates) their presence in the bottom of the pool remained difficult to explain. In addition, a collection of scattered animal bones in the bottom of the pool included unusually high numbers of red deer antlers and dog bones. From the same position, but even more significant, came the facial part of a human skull (*Fig 28*). This retained evidence that, before deposition, it had been deliberately cut from the rest of the cranium.

Although a 'ritual' interpretation is rightly regarded as an archaeological cliché to explain the inexplicable, all this evidence points to one remarkable conclusion: that the monument known as the King's Stables was constructed in the Late Bronze Age as a pool for ritual purposes. This

28 *Human skull.*

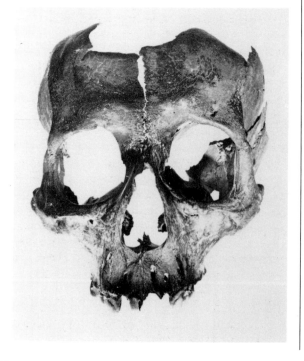

suggestion can be supported by comparison with sites in Britain and on the Continent. In later prehistoric times the people of north-west Europe worshipped at sacred groves and springs, and here cult practices, like auguries and sacrifices to local deities, are known to have taken place. Much of our Late Bronze Age metalwork comes from rivers, lakes and bogs, and these pieces may represent offerings to water spirits. But in Ireland the King's Stables remains the only purpose-built monument which we can suggest, on the evidence of excavation, anticipates the mass of early Irish tradition which attests to veneration of sacred pools, severed head cults, animal sacrifice and votive offerings.

When the trial excavation was completed and the trenches were filled in the owner generously agreed not to drain the monument, as this would eventually have destroyed all of the important organic material still preserved in its interior. This small excavation was dramatically successful in demonstrating the antiquity and unique nature of the site, in underlining the ritual aspects of the whole Navan Fort area and, finally, in helping to ensure the preservation of the monument. Late in 1987 we can report that this important site has just been acquired by the Department of the Environment and has passed into State care.

CJL

Lynn, C J, 'Trial excavations at The King's Stables, Tray townland, County Armagh', *Ulster J Archaeol* 30 (1977), 42–62.

12. THE IRON AGE GATES OF ULSTER?

THE DORSEY
Co Armagh

H 948193
Scheduled

The series of large earthworks known as 'the Dorsey' lies in south Armagh, 2 km north-west of Silver Bridge on the main road from Newtownhamilton to Dundalk.* The earthworks are often described as an enclosure, with a perimeter of 4.3 km (2.7 miles) and a very irregular rectangular plan which is largely determined by the local topography (*Fig 29*). Much of the earthworks and stretches of piling across boggy areas have been destroyed, but parts of the plan can be filled in from old maps and air photographs. Other lengths of the perimeter, totalling about a quarter, have to be completed from guesswork.

The main surviving parts of the Dorsey lie on the south side in two separate sections, each comprising a single massive embankment with a deep ditch on either side (*Fig 30*). The top of the central bank is about 8 m higher than the ditch bottoms. The main earthworks cut off the ends of two ridges and appear to have been linked originally by further sinuous banks and a structure containing massive oak piles which ran across the intervening bog.

It is possible that these remarkable earthworks were made to cut off one of the few ancient routeways from the south into the plain of Armagh and to channel traffic through an original causeway or gate in the eastern section of the earthwork (the name Dorsey means 'the gates'). The northern section, which appears to have been of relatively slight proportions, runs in an irregular loop from near the outer ends of the large southern sections. This creates an enormous 'enclosure' in a broken landscape, containing boggy hollows, smooth ridges, streams, and low, rocky knolls. It is not, therefore, possible to view the whole circuit from a single vantage point.

The Dorsey has puzzled generations of antiquarians and archaeologists for, despite a series of

---

* The earthworks lie in the townlands of Tullynavall and Dorsy but the monument itself has usually been written as 'the Dorsey', with an e.

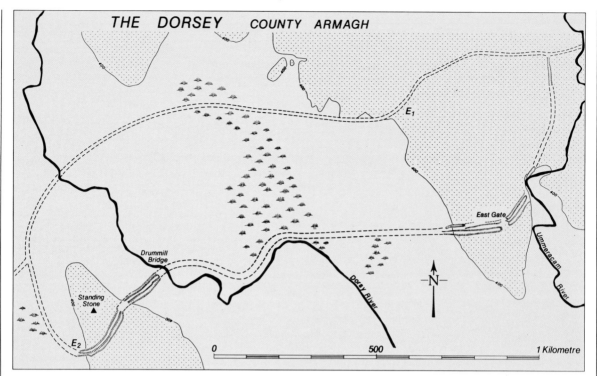

29 Plan of the Dorsey.

30 Earthworks on south-east.

trial excavations in the late 1930s, no object or structure had ever been found which could give clear evidence for its date or purpose. In the 1930s a number of 'piles' or heavy beams of shaped timber were discovered in boggy ground at the south-west corner of the earthworks, and a series of stake-holes and gullies, possibly representing the site of a gate-keeper's hut, was found immediately east of the gap in the large earthwork at the south-east. But earlier workers lacked the important facilities of radiocarbon analysis and dendrochronology for dating charcoal and timber, and the age of the monument remained a mystery.

Early in 1977 a farm access was widened in the north-east section of the enclosure and the edge of a layer of charcoal and burnt soil was exposed under the slight remains of the ancient embankment. A small excavation was organized immediately to expose enough charcoal to allow radiocarbon dating of the burnt layer and to determine its relationship to the earthwork (*Fig 29, E1*). The excavation showed that the charcoal represented the remains of a substantial timber palisade which was covered by the bank immediately after it had burned down. This was an important discovery because it meant that, for the first time, an estimate of the date of this part of the earthwork, within a century either way, could be made. But the happy expectation of radiocarbon dating was rapidly surpassed by a remarkable series of coincidences.

One warm evening, members of the small excavation team decided to walk all around the perimeter of the Dorsey, as several of the assistants had not seen it before. On reaching the south-west corner they discovered, with a mixture of dismay and excitement, that bulldozing for land reclamation had started at the bottom of the field in which piles were uncovered in 1938–9. Evidently work had only started that same day and the tops of rotted ancient oak posts (preserved in the boggy ground) were visible in the disturbed surface, with the bulldozer parked for the night nearby. Fortunately, the owner of the field, who was unaware of the existence of the piles, suspended work and the excavation team quickly transferred to the new site (*Fig 29, E2*). The timbers, set side by side in a shallow trench, represented the remains of a palisade of roughly-squared oak posts (*Fig 31*). The trench was traced for a length of some 60 m and it ran parallel to, and inside (north of), the line of a

31 *Palisade of oak posts.*

filled-up ditch which formed part of the south-west corner of the main Dorsey earthworks. The upright posts were wedged in the slot with horizontal boards of oak and there was evidence that the palisade may have been propped at intervals, as a few traces of timbers lying at right angles to the palisade on the ground surface were found. These could represent collapsed parts of the palisade or supports for sloping braces. Some of the post-butts had holes cut in them, either to facilitate dragging into position or indicating that they had originally been used in another structure.

The discovery of this palisade underlines the strongly defensive character of the Dorsey. Its builders were not content to rely on the patch of wet bog for defence of the south-west corner but augmented the edge of the morass with the ditch and a stout palisade. But the fortunate coincidences did not end with this discovery. A dendrochronological examination of the oak posts by Dr M Baillie of Queen's University Palaeoecology Centre showed that all the timbers had been cut down in the same year, and that it was the *same year* as for the felling of the timbers of the large wooden structure, possibly a ceremonial building, found in excavations carried out in the 1960s by D M Waterman at Navan Fort, 27 km to the north. The conclusion was, therefore, that the most intriguing part of the structural sequence at Navan Fort and part, at least, of the Dorsey were constructed at exactly the same time and presumably by the same population group.

Several months after the excavation finished the results of the radiocarbon dating of the samples of charred palisade from the north-east side showed that the timbers had probably been growing between about 380 BC and AD 25, indicating that the palisade was constructed in the Iron Age. In 1983, however, Dr Baillie completed his links of overlapping tree-ring patterns and was able to state with certainty that the timbers from the Dorsey (and the Navan Fort structure) were all cut down *a few years after 100 BC*.

Earlier writers had associated the Dorsey with Navan Fort on tenuous evidence, but the relationship has now been confirmed by the results of these small excavations at the Dorsey and by the subsequent laboratory analysis. The work shows, however, that the major activity at both sites took place about 400 years *earlier* than had been suggested on historical grounds. It is likely that the Dorsey was constructed as a routeway defence for the political or tribal area which had Navan Fort as its capital. Radiocarbon dates from a burnt palisade in the Worm Ditch, a linear earthwork further west in Co Monaghan, show that it too was built at about the same time as the Dorsey. This supports the suggestion that several, or all, of the scattered lengths of earthwork in south Ulster were built at about the same time as part of a system of frontier demarcation, or for defence at vulnerable points on a boundary.

Until recent years a sizeable archaeological team could have spent many seasons excavating around the Dorsey and might still have failed to find any datable artifacts in a suitable context to reveal the date of the earthwork. In the 1970s tree-ring dating allowed the date of the site to be worked out for the first time, and showed that it was of *exactly* the same age as the most important timber structure excavated at Navan Fort. This depended on the discovery of the exposed timber piles, which in turn depended on the rare chance of a group of archaeologists being in the area *and* on the chance that they should go for a stroll to that place on that particular evening. A day earlier and there would have been no sign that bulldozing was planned; a day later and the evidence, which might not survive elsewhere, would have been unwittingly destroyed.

CJL

Lynn, C J, 'The Dorsey and other linear earthworks', in Scott, B G (ed) *Studies on Early Ireland: Essays in Honour of M V Duignan* (Belfast, 1980) 121–128.

13. AN ENIGMA SOLVED

KILTIERNEY
Co Fermanagh

H 217626

Scheduled

The large mound in Kiltierney Deerpark has long been a puzzling site. It had been the subject of several excavations over the past hundred years, but remained an enigma. The recent work, in 1983–4, was done because the landowner wished to remove part of the monument, but happily, as a result of the excavation and subsequent negotiation, the site is to survive intact.

Kiltierney Deerpark is a large tract of land which remained unenclosed (except for the Deerpark wall) and relatively unchanged until the early 1970s. The excavated site is part of a complex of Neolithic and Bronze Age monuments which must have formed an important early 'necropolis' in the rolling limestone terrain. Surviving to the late 19th century and described (in 1881) by W F Wakeman

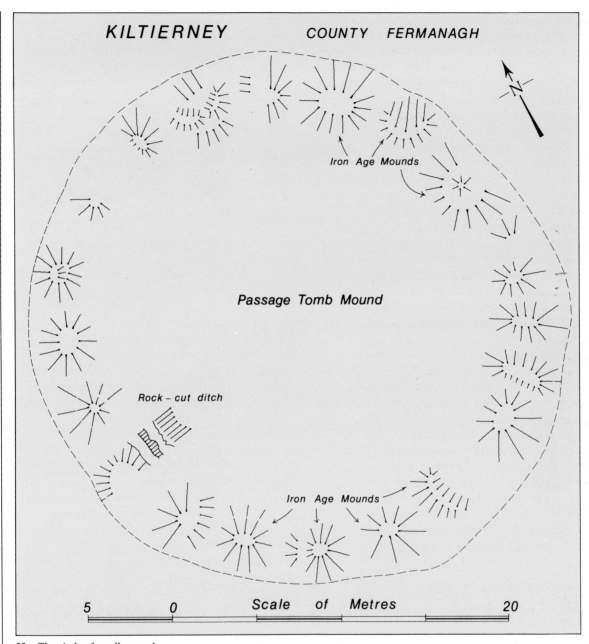

KILTIERNEY   COUNTY FERMANAGH

Iron Age Mounds

Passage Tomb Mound

Rock – cut ditch

Iron Age Mounds

5   0   Scale   of   Metres   20

32   *The circle of small mounds.*

were 'nine mounds of important dimensions besides a considerable number of lesser tumuli, and at least one stone circle'. The threatened site survived as a mound, 20 m in diameter and 1.5 m high. It is in origin a Neolithic passage tomb, and two of its large stones with distinctive pocked decoration now lie on top of the mound. It is thought that the passage and burial chamber were destroyed by a 19th-century excavation. Round

the mound was a slight ditch, 3 m wide and 1 m deep, and surrounding this was a circle of 21 small mounds, averaging 3 m in diameter and 1 m high, which had always been something of an enigma (*Fig 32*).

It was these small mounds that were in danger of removal. At least half of these 'satellite' mounds had been excavated, on at least three previous occasions, in unsuccessful attempts to find out what they were, as there is no other site known exactly like this in Ireland. It was not until the rescue excavation of 1983–4 that the mounds finally yielded up their secret. The discovery of an Iron Age cremation burial under one of the small mounds suggested that they covered an Iron Age cremation cemetery. After more than 2000 years the Neolithic passage tomb had been remodelled to become the centre-piece of an unusual Iron Age ring-barrow.

The Iron Age alterations involved the digging of a ditch round the base of the Neolithic mound. The clay and broken limestone produced were partly used to add to the passage tomb mound, and some Iron Age cremation burials were inserted in the mound in shallow pits. Several of these burials had come to light during excavations done in 1969, and provided the first evidence for Iron Age activity here. The 1969 finds included a bronze fibula or 'safety-pin' brooch and four glass beads.

Cremated bones were also placed on the old ground surface on the outside edge of the new ditch and were covered with small mounds of clay and limestone. The symmetry of the arrangement strongly suggests that the satellite mounds were laid out in a single operation, rather than built over a long period. Excavation showed that there were originally nineteen (not 21) small mounds. About half had been previously examined and there were reports of the finding of bone, but the early reports are not full enough to tell us if all the mounds covered burials. As part of the recent work several of the disturbed mounds were re-examined, but one fragment of green glass and a small piece of cremated bone were the only finds from these.

Excavation of the undisturbed mound produced a cremation burial, together with an iron fibula brooch of the 1st century AD (*Fig 33*), the only complete iron example so far found in Ireland, other iron fragments and pieces of broken bronze objects, some decorated in a distinctively Iron Age style, with cast features and enamelled settings. The most important of the bronze finds, a cast fragment with lobed decoration, an enamel setting and a groove to receive another element, is probably part of a mirror handle, of the type commonly used by Celts and Romans.

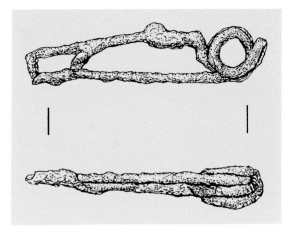

33   *Iron fibula (drawing D Warner).*

The fact that the objects were fragmented and only a small part of any one object was found requires an explanation. Perhaps only a token amount of material from the cremation pyre was taken to the burial site, or perhaps loss was inevitable in the scraping up of the burned residue of the fire. Another possibility is that the cremated remains were divided into many parts, each deposited under a separate mound. Future excavation of the remaining undisturbed mounds could provide further clues for this new aspect of the Kiltierney puzzle.

Iron Age burials are rare in Ireland: some twenty sites have so far produced them. The majority have come from flat cemeteries or newly-built monuments, such as ring-barrows. Apart from the Kiltierney example, only two other cases are known of Iron Age burials inserted into earlier monuments, at Carrowbeg North and Pollacorragune, both in Co Galway and both into Bronze Age mounds. It is interesting to speculate that the reuse of earlier sites happened in some emergency, perhaps after a battle or a natural catastrophe, when both time and manpower were for some reason short. But this is one enigma for which we may never have the answer.

CF

Davies, O, 'The cairn in Castle Archdale Deer-park', *Ulster J Archaeol* 9 (1946), 54–7.

DUNMISK   H 628706
Co Tyrone   Scheduled

About 2 km south-east of Carrickmore in mid Tyrone the hill of Dunmisk stands enigmatically above the Camowen valley (*Fig 34*). Its flat top and terraced slope clearly show it has been modified by man. The Ordnance Survey named it as a fort, local legend as a fairy hill, but both were wrong.

The chance to establish the date and nature of this unusual monument came in 1984, when the area was threatened by a gravel quarry. The results of a trial excavation were so surprising and rewarding that a major excavation was undertaken over the summers of 1984 and 1985, concluded in 1986. On top of this isolated and weather-beaten hill were found, contrary to all expectations, the remains of a previously unknown Early Christian ecclesiastical site and a graveyard of quite extraordinary size and complexity (*Fig 35*).

By 1986 over 400 graves had been excavated (*Fig 36*). In the central part of the site these were neatly arranged and spaced around a large pit, which perhaps once held a wooden cross. To the east the graves were dug in a complex series of chains, each head-to-toe with its neighbours. So densely packed and intercut were these burials that after excavation virtually nothing remained, just a large hole with occasional remnants of undisturbed earth where by chance no graves had been dug.

In the south-east corner of the site the graves were even more densely packed, and were frequently cut one across another. Sometimes there were even distinct layers of graves, with one series of large deep burials, overlain by a second series of small shallow ones (often child burials). Grave markers were found in this area. Sometimes these took the form of slabs of stone set around the grave edges and at other times a carefully prepared layer of white cobbles over the grave.

The south-east quadrant seemed to be a much favoured choice of burial site, and to contain more elaborate (and perhaps important) burials. The reason for this became clear when the remains of large and carefully constructed post-sockets and trenches, perhaps designed to hold wooden beams, were discovered, all that survived of a substantial timber building. In all probability this was an early church.

The anatomical study of the human remains has yet to be completed but will in due course give a detailed picture of the physique and health of an Early Christian population. Already it can be determined that the average age of death was about 25 years, and that only 2.5 per cent of the population survived until the age of 40, while about 25 per cent died before the age of 15. The wear and decay of the teeth suggest a mixed diet of meat and cereals, with very little in the way of sweeteners (probably only honey): in fact only 12.5 per cent of the teeth showed signs of dental caries, compared with anything up to 90 per cent in a modern population.

In addition to the probable church and this extensive burial ground two areas of craft activities were found, one solely concerned with metalworking, the other with both metal and glass. It is this evidence which suggests that the site was occupied by a monastic community, and was not just a church site and burial ground. A small number of glass rods and millefiori glass settings were found amongst the more mundane industrial debris of slag, crucibles and broken moulds, and it comes as some surprise to find such fine quality

34 Dunmisk from the north.

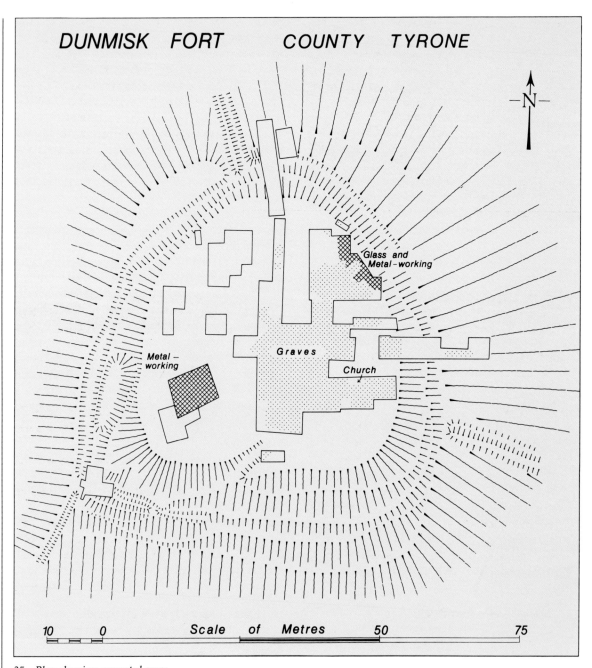

DUNMISK FORT   COUNTY TYRONE

N

Glass and
Metal-working

Metal-
working

Graves

Church

10   0   Scale of Metres   50   75

35 *Plan showing excavated areas.*

28

36   *Some of the excavated graves.*

pieces in this apparently remote spot at such an early date. But perhaps it is no more surprising than the nature and date of the site itself.

The *Tripartite Life of St Patrick*, written in about 900, refers to a now lost church called *Domnach Mescáin* (the Brewer's Church). Could Dunmisk be a corruption of *Domnach Mescáin* (*dún*, fort, for *domnach*, church), and this hilltop be the site of a long-abandoned and forgotten early foundation, going back even to the 5th century?

RJI

15. THE LEANING WALL

ST JOHN'S POINT CHURCH
Co Down

J 527338

State care

St John's Point church stands near the shore on the south-east tip of the Lecale peninsula. It is a small stone building, just over 7 m long and 5 m wide. Probably built in the 10th or 11th century, the church is now roofless and lacks most of the east gable, but preserves the distinctive pre-Romanesque features of *antae* (short masonry extensions beyond the gables) and west door with sloping jambs (*Fig 37*). Conservation work on the church, which is in State care, focused attention on the pronounced lean of the north wall, and two

small trenches were excavated in 1977, on either side of its footings, to search for possible causes of the trouble.

Not surprisingly, burials were quickly encountered. The earliest, a stone cist which ran obliquely under the wall (*Fig 38*), and two others close by, clearly pre-dated the stone church, a feature paralleled in the 1961 excavation at the Derry Churches on the Ards peninsula. There an Early Christian cist cemetery and an early stone and timber building, possibly a church, were

37   *View of church from north-west.*

38   *Stone cist appearing under church wall.*

shown to pre-date the two stone churches. While no early timber church was found in the small trenches at St John's Point, it is a fair assumption that one existed and awaits discovery by further excavation.

The 26 graves found in the church were extensively intercut but it was only possible to distinguish some relative sequences of burials. No doubt the earliest inhumations, all of adult males, belonged to the years following the building of the stone church. But they were all simple Christian burials, lacking cists, coffins or grave-goods, and precise dating was not possible.

One grave, however, containing the remains of a teenage boy, was of particular interest. Two white quartz pebbles had been deliberately placed with the corpse, one behind the head and the other between the legs, near the groin. The phenomenon of white stones associated with Early Christian burials has been noted frequently throughout the British Isles. One antiquarian argued that the custom arose from a Biblical passage: 'I [God] . . . will give him a white stone, and in the stone a new name written, which no one knoweth but he that receiveth' (Revelation, ch ii, v 17), though it is difficult to see how this can be reconciled with the discovery of more than one stone in a grave. White stones have also been found with prehistoric, non-Christian burials, suggesting that this is perhaps a tradition which was 'adopted' by Christianity, and one which unthinkingly persists today in the white chippings which mark so many graves.

The discovery, just below the surface inside the church, of the graves of two babies is a reminder that churches which have fallen into disuse as places of worship may yet retain a role in the cycle of life and death. The burial of infants who died before receiving baptism resulted in the creation of children's graveyards in parts of Ireland, and arrangements were also made for the burial of people whose religious credentials were doubtful, such as suicides, strangers, or shipwrecked sailors washed ashore. It is possible, given the location of the church on a dangerous coastline, that some of the burials found in the upper soil levels (and thus latest in date) may have been in this last category. But without clues provided by clothing, and on the anatomical evidence alone, such an interpretation must remain speculative.

NFB

Brannon, N F, 'A trial excavation at St John's Point Church, County Down', *Ulster J Archaeol* 43 (1980), 59–64.
Waterman, D M, 'The Early Christian churches and cemetery at Derry, Co Down', *Ulster J Archaeol* 30 (1967), 53–75.

16. UNEXPECTED WOODEN SOUTERRAIN

COOLCRAN
Co Fermanagh

H 365500

Souterrains are artificial underground chambers or passages of the Early Christian period, normally built of stone or cut from rock. They are found widely in Ireland, but their distribution is uneven. Topographical factors have been suggested to explain their absence from some areas, such as mountainous terrain or bogland, or perhaps heavy forest cover. During a recent archaeological survey of Co Fermanagh one of the puzzles was the almost complete absence of souterrains in an area where monuments of the Early Christian period were otherwise well represented. An answer was unexpectedly found during the rescue excavation of a hilltop rath at Coolcran, near Tempo, in 1983. This produced evidence for a souterrain, built not in the conventional manner with drystone walls and a stone lintelled roof, but with oak posts and wattlework (*Fig 39*).

On the eastern side of the rath a narrow outlet cut 1.2 m deep into the subsoil ran for 6.5 m from

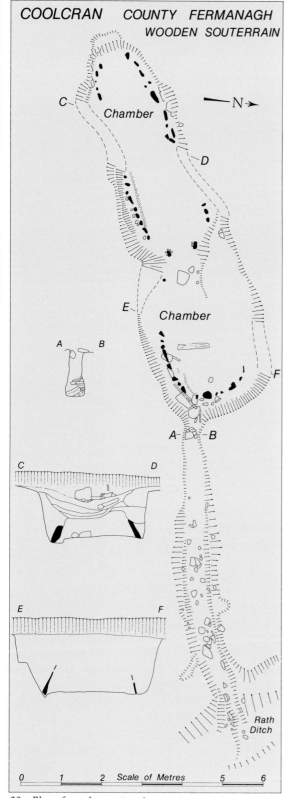

COOLCRAN COUNTY FERMANAGH
WOODEN SOUTERRAIN

N→

Chamber

C

D

E

Chamber

A
B

F

A—B

C
D

E
F

A—B

Rath
Ditch

0   1   2   Scale of Metres   5   6

39   Plan of wooden souterrain.

40   Looking into east end of chamber.

the surrounding ditch towards the centre of the site, where it joined a timber-lined chamber. At the point of contact with the chamber the outlet had been deliberately blocked with stones in antiquity. The chamber was a large sub-rectangular pit, 9 m long, 3.5 m wide, cut with vertical sides into the subsoil to a depth of 1.3 m. Around the edge of the flat-bottomed pit were 48 oak timbers. They were set directly on the bottom of the pit and sloped inwards at an angle of about 30 degrees from vertical (*Fig 40*). Fortunately the wood was preserved because the level of the water-table was high enough to provide suitable conditions for survival, and the wooden fragments varied from 0.2 to 0.6 m in height, while the outlines of rotted posts were observed in some places continuing at the same pitch. Evidence was found of saw-cuts on the timbers, but there was no sign of axe-marks. A thin, dark grey organic line was seen to run around and between the timbers and this was interpreted as the remains of wattle walling. A constriction in the chamber close to a pair of stout timber uprights

31

set in stone-packed post-holes seemed to indicate a division into two parts. Examination of thirteen of the timbers provided a dendrochronological date of AD 822 ± 9 and showed that some of the timbers in both chambers were from the same tree.

Though this technique of building a souterrain – with wooden uprights and wattle infilling – had not previously been recorded, the Coolcran structure, entirely unsuspected before excavation, must be a souterrain. It is now reasonable to sug-

gest that the building of wooden souterrains may have been common in Co Fermanagh – and perhaps in other areas, where there were puzzling blanks on the distribution maps.

BBW

Lucas, A T, 'Souterrains: the literary evidence', *Béaloideas* 39–41 (1971–3), 165–91.
Williams, B B, 'Excavation of a rath at Coolcran, County Fermanagh', *Ulster J Archaeol* 48 (1985), 69–80.

17. A THOUSAND YEAR-OLD FARM

BALLYWEE   J 218899
Co Antrim   State care

This large site was excavated in 1974 because of its threatened removal in a farm improvement scheme. The complex was first described in the 1838 Ordnance Survey Memoir of the Parish of Donegore as a 'cyclopean fort', that is, one with large stones in its ramparts. It was noted that 'About ten years ago an attempt to cultivate the interior of the fort and to level some of the ramparts was made by a man . . . who lived within a few yards of it, but this was attended by his wife's partially losing her intellects which she has not yet recovered. The fort, therefore, is likely to remain in its present state'. The site does indeed appear to have survived undisturbed since the 1830s, apart from the demolition of its souterrains. The archaeologists worked in 1974 without fear, however, on the assumption that the excavation would be regarded as constructive by the local fairies. Nevertheless, an isolated thorn tree growing in the middle of an Early Christian building was avoided until it fell by itself! Evidence for the abortive earlier attempt at cultivation was recovered in the form of a series of parallel, shallow trenches in the centre and east of the site. It is possible that the west side was avoided because of the number of large stones immediately below the surface (the remains of Early Christian structures) rather than because of anxiety about possible retribution.

Before excavation it was clear that the Bally-

wee settlement was well preserved and an area of some 1500 sq m was examined (*Fig 41*). It was necessary to remove little more than the topsoil to expose the foundations of as many as nine Early Christian period buildings and three souterrains.

The site lies in a small boggy field, 2 km north of Parkgate, on the east slope of Donegore Hill, at an altitude of over 150 m. There are several small springs immediately upslope and before excavation a small stream ran through the site from north-west to south-east. While the location may have been chosen with access to water in mind this may have caused drainage problems and it seems likely that the low external banks, which can be roughly described as two joined semicircles on plan (85 m in overall diameter) on the uphill side, were designed to deflect run-off water rather than to provide a serious defence. In this account, therefore, we avoid calling the site a rath or ring-fort, which implies a farmstead surrounded by a bank of uniform proportions, although it is clearly related to raths and cashels.

The site and the structures revealed by excavation are described in summary, in the manner of a conducted tour, with reference to *Fig 41*.

The main entrance to the settlement was a simple gap in the encircling low bank retained on each side by kerbs of boulders. The bank survived only on the west; the perimeter of the site was a

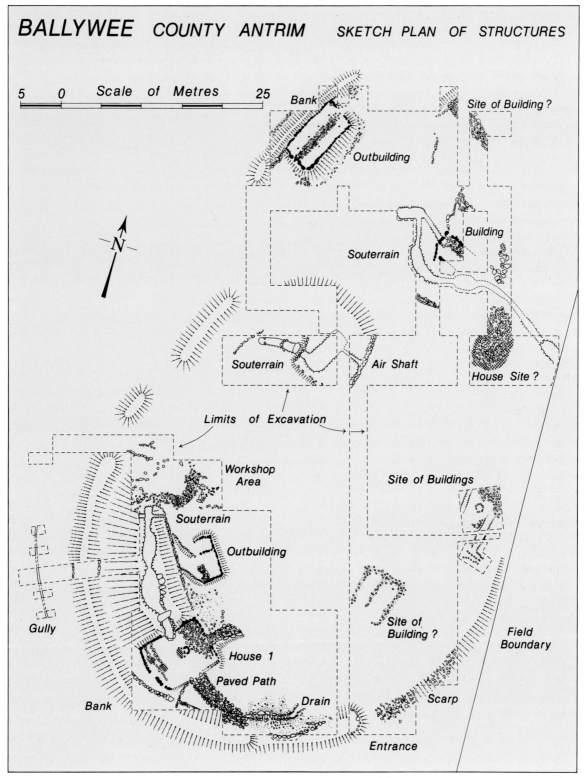

BALLYWEE COUNTY ANTRIM   SKETCH PLAN OF STRUCTURES

5   0   Scale of Metres   25

N

Bank

Site of Building ?

Outbuilding

Building

Souterrain

Souterrain

Air Shaft

House Site ?

Limits of Excavation

Workshop Area

Souterrain

Site of Buildings

Outbuilding

Gully

Site of Building ?

Field Boundary

House 1

Bank

Paved Path

Drain

Scarp

Entrance

41   General plan.

slight stone-strewn slope on the south-east. A stone-lined open drain ran downslope towards the entrance and carried run-off from a 2 m-wide paved path which, like many other features on the site, was neatly delimited by slightly raised kerbs of stones. The path led directly into a substantial rectangular house. This was 7 by 4 m internally and the bases of three of its walls were composed of turves retained by kerbs of upright boulders on the faces (*Fig 42*). The fourth wall, on the south, was indicated by a double row of small boulders, probably packing for a wall of timber or wicker-work. The house had a central fireplace, delimited by boulders, and a paved side entrance. This building could be confidently identified as a dwelling because of the amount of occupation debris – potsherds, charcoal, iron objects, beads, bronze pins and a quern fragment – found in and around it. A place of refuge was provided by a souterrain, some 16 m long, entered from inside the north end of the house. The souterrain stood within a broad bank and was roofed with massive lintels, most of which had been broken and lay on the floor. There was a stone-lined ventilation shaft at the north end.

The bank covering the souterrain was retained on the downhill side by a wall of boulders about 1 m high. Near this, at the edge of the open interior of the settlement, was a small outbuilding with substantial wall footings of stone and turf on three sides but closed only by two widely-spaced, slanting, flimsy rows of boulders on the west. This structure lacked a hearth and may have been used as a workshop or store. At the north end of the souterrain there was a broad semicircle of heavy paving. This was disturbed on the north but could represent either the outline of a roofed structure or an open-air working area. Red-burnt soil, charcoal and a few fragments of crucibles for melting bronze were found among the loose stones at its centre.

At the north side of the main enclosure excavation of an isolated low mound showed that it covered another souterrain, this time intact, comprising a single large chamber with an air-shaft on the east. The chamber was entered by a stone-lined

42 *Excavation of principal house, showing hearth in centre and souterrain entrance behind.*

34

vertical drop and chute on the west. This replaced a longer chute which was shortened by the insertion of the drop-hole, presumably to accommodate the souterrain entrance to a rebuilt surface structure, only vague traces of which survived. The upper edge of the flat-topped mound containing the souterrain was delimited by a kerb of boulders laid end-to-end. Neat stone kerbing of this type, not recorded to the same extent at any other excavated site, is typical of the structures at Ballywee.

Apart from vague traces of two other rectilinear buildings at the south-east, now covered in, this represents the extent of the excavation of the larger enclosure. The undulating traces of the settlement continued further north and the 1838 OS Memoir indicated that a smaller enclosure was appended here to form a rough figure-of-eight on plan. The most prominent surviving feature was a small rectilinear platform built against the inside of an arc of low bank on the north-west. On excavation this turned out to be the base for a rectangular structure, measuring 10 by 5 m and defined by a kerb of boulders at the edge of the platform. A paved path, flanked by post-holes, ran along the whole length of the centre of the building which was entered at the north end. The only finds from it were two small iron knife-blades, which turned up just inside the entrance. The structure was an outbuilding, probably a storehouse, as there was no hearth, no occupation debris and the spaces on either side of the axial path seemed too small to have served as animal stalls. Although the plans of this and other buildings were well defined it is not possible to be certain how the walls and roofs of the structures were built.

Traces of the sites of other buildings were found in this 'northern annexe' (which may not have been a complete enclosure), such as the well-preserved set of wall-footings for a building partly excavated on the east. At the north-west end of this structure there was an access-hole to a long and tortuous souterrain. This was badly damaged but the walls of several large chambers survive (precariously) and there are traces of the narrow connecting passages. In the topsoil, between the east end of the souterrain and an area of paving possibly representing a house site, a beautifully decorated silvered bronze buckle was found (*Fig 43*).

All the buildings and souterrains noted above were exposed immediately below the topsoil and it

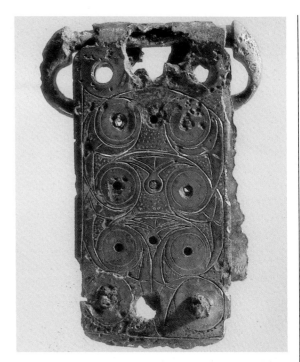

43 *Silver-plated bronze buckle with incised decoration and blue glass studs (height 4.9 cm).*

is likely that all were broadly contemporary. In some places, however, where excavation penetrated lower there were traces of an earlier phase of occupation, still in the Early Christian period, in which structures of timber or wicker were used.

As a result of the 1974 excavation the initial threat receded and the site is now in State care. It is undergoing progressive small-scale conservation for presentation to the public as time and resources permit. When consolidation is finished this will be the only site in Northern Ireland where the visitor will be able to see substantial remains of the foundations of a number of Early Christian houses and outbuildings associated with good examples of souterrains. The remains of similar farming settlements are still fairly common (raths or ring-forts) and many others have been excavated in advance of destruction. But elsewhere the traces of structures, which were mainly of wickerwork, have been too fragile to contemplate preservation. The Ballywee settlement typifies, in a robust form, the picture of an Early Christian settlement, with enclosures, dwellings, outbuildings and souterrains, which can be constructed from other excavations and from early documentary sources.

CJL

BALLYUTOAG
Co Antrim

J 274796

Settlement of the Early Christian period in Ireland is well represented by the thousands of raths, circular earthen enclosed farmsteads, which dot the lowland areas. These raths, popularly known as forts or 'forths', have survived through many centuries of desertion, largely because of traditional taboos but perhaps also because they presented too big an obstacle to remove. Unfortunately their fields and related structures have long ago been cleared away in successive

44   Area plan with ancient features bold.

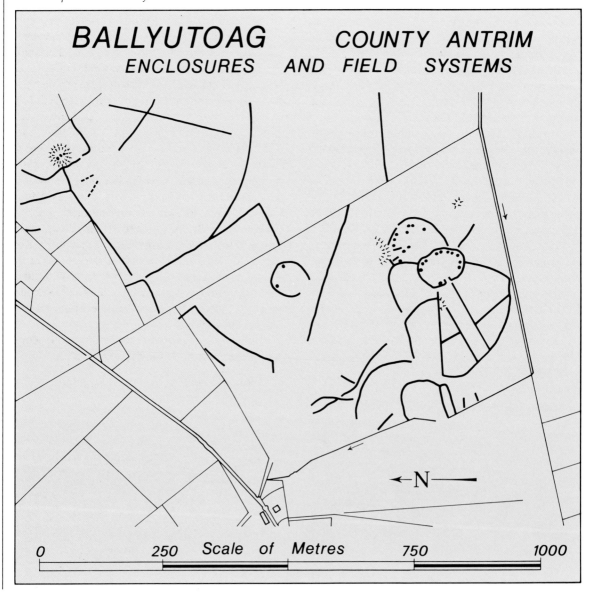

reorganizations of the land. From the great density of rath distribution in south Antrim, however, it is clear that much of the land must have been enclosed; indeed the proverb 'Good fences make good neighbours' would have been well understood in this period, with its precise legal requirements governing the erection and maintenance of fences.

The archaeology of the uplands has been less intensively explored in the past than the lowlands, but recently interesting new discoveries have been made on the hills of County Antrim in the course of an archaeological survey, in which air photographs have been used systematically to search for new sites. In remote and inaccessible uplands the photos have helped to locate many new sites including types which have rarely been identified before. Whole farms, with their dwelling houses, animal pens, fields, cultivation ridges and clearance cairns, lie deserted on the hillsides, often between 240 and 275 metres above sea-level, just beyond the margins of modern agriculture.

The first of these upland settlements to be found in the recent survey was an extensive complex of fields associated both with a rath and other curvilinear settlement enclosures at Ballyutoag, some 8 km north-west of Belfast (Fig 44). In 1981 a small research excavation was undertaken to try to find out something about this 'new' type of settlement and, in particular, to try to discover its date. Working on the assumption that small grassy mounds set just within the banks of the enclosures were house platforms, first a trial trench and then all of one mound were excavated followed by trenches across two others. Excavation confirmed that these were the remains of houses, and the fully excavated house, rebuilt four times, was dated by radiocarbon to the 8th century (Fig 45). The picture which emerged was of an Early Christ-

ian upland village of 23 houses, with accommodation for perhaps 100 people or even more, if all the houses were occupied at the same time.

Cultivation ridges show that crops were grown, and charred remains of barley, oats and wheat were found preserved in the domestic hearths. Finds were numerous but limited to coarse pottery and chips of flint, together with the stem of a bronze ringed pin and a fragment of a lignite bracelet. Pottery may have been made on site, as we found a lump of clay which had been squeezed in the hand and then accidentally fired, perhaps with the pottery vessels. The fine set of fingerprints fired in the clay were from the right hand of a teenager.

Whether the occupation at Ballyutoag was permanent or seasonal is not clear: the excavation did not provide conclusive evidence. Perhaps the climate was warmer and drier than today and permanent occupation was possible on these high slopes, now exposed and often cloud-covered. But we know that transhumance, the seasonal movement of herds and people to upland pastures, was of great economic importance in Early Christian Ireland. There are documentary references to women going to the herds in the mountains, to youths herding cattle in the mountains, and to the *macha samraid*, the summer milking place in the hills. As the site at Ballyutoag is so strikingly different in situation from the better known lowland raths, and had the potential to house a large community rather than an extended family, it seems possible that this may indeed have been a transhumance village in the upland summer pastures (Fig 46).

Subsequent fieldwork in Antrim has confirmed that curvilinear fields are found associated

46 Summertime at Ballyutoag? (drawing S Shaw).

45 House platform during excavation.

with upland raths, and quite a number of 'villages' of the Ballyutoag type have now been located in the hills. Traces of medieval agriculture and settlement have also begun to emerge. Houses of the medieval period have been elusive in Ireland, but recent field survey in Antrim, together with several excavations by Nick Brannon (*see p 70*),

Philip Robinson and the present writer, suggest that there are many medieval settlement sites waiting to be found in the uplands

BBW

Williams, B B, 'Excavations at Ballyutoag, County Antrim', *Ulster J Archaeol* 47 (1984), 37–49.

19. THE STORY IN A MOUND

GRANSHA   J 531769
Co Down   Scheduled

This is the first of four accounts of excavations on layered mounds. These can be seen as a planned series of investigations of a particularly interesting and complex type of site, of which there may be several hundred in Northern Ireland, even though the work in each case was carried out in response to threatened destruction.

The mound at Gransha stands 1.3 km south of Six-Road-Ends, between Bangor and Newtownards, at the east side of a low drumlin with flat, formerly boggy, land further to the east. It was 6 m high before excavation and some 45 m in diameter

at the base. Its flat top was oval in plan, 20 by 24 m, and there was no trace of the usual encircling ditch at the base (*Fig 47*). This impressive monument was thought either to be a motte (castle mound) dating from the period of the Anglo-Norman settlement of the late 12th century, or a raised or platform-type rath of the preceding Early Christian period.

In 1972 it was reported that a small quarry had been opened in the east side of the mound and this had exposed layers of artificial build-up running right through the mound. Pottery, boulders, char-

47   The mound before excavation from east (photo E M Griffith).

38

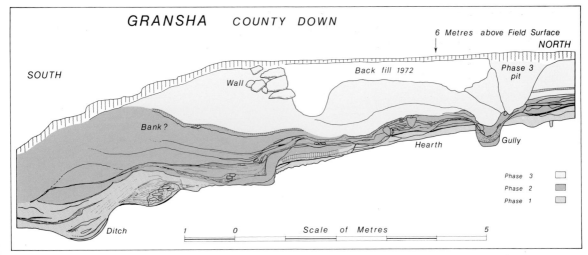

48   Vertical section through south side of mound.

coal and animal bones fell out of various parts of the crumbling and irregular vertical section. It was immediately clear that the mound was *not* a single-period motte, and all the pottery recovered from the loose scree was of Early Christian date. The likelihood remained, however, that the mound was remodelled and occupied in its final phase by the Anglo-Normans who had often been shown to have adapted earlier earthworks as defended sites.

This stratified mound was obviously important, and a small excavation was organized in 1972 to examine those parts in danger of collapse and to consolidate the steep edges of the quarry, the owner having agreed not to disturb the mound in future. A further small investigation was necessary in 1982 when part of the mound began to slip but the remnant is now stable.

The layers uncovered were very complicated and, because of the small area examined, were difficult to interpret fully. It will be best to summarize the growth of the mound (the physical evidence) and the history of activity on it (our interpretation) in chronological order, from the bottom upwards, that is, the direct reverse of the sequence of excavation, from the top down. The evolution of the mound can be divided into three major phases of different activity, recognizable from variations in the succession of layers accumulating or dumped on the site (*Fig 48*).

Phase 1

A small gravel ridge about 4.5 m high occupied the site before settlement began in the Early Christian period. Around AD 600 a small ditch, about 1.5 m wide and 1 m deep, was cut on the lower slopes of the natural ridge. This may have formed a complete enclosure, oval in plan. Immediately above the ditch was a low bank, surmounted by a brushwood fence or hedge. This brief period of occupation, in which the mound may have been used as a temporary stronghold, ended with the burning of the perimeter timberwork. Only two finds were recovered at this level, both from the ditch fill. One was a small, bronze, zoomorphic (animal-like) penannular brooch, badly corroded, with enamel and millefiori glass in the terminals (*Fig 49*). The other was a wheel-thrown jar of a type known as 'E ware', which was imported to western Britain and Ireland from Gaul around AD 600. These finds indicate that the occupants of the hillock at this stage were of above average status. After the burning of its defences the mound may have been abandoned for a short period.

Phase 2

The still largely natural profile of the mound and the outline of the ditch and bank were submerged during this phase by the accumulation of a thick deposit of alternating occupation layers and thin dumps of clean soil. This series of layers clearly represented fairly continuous settlement on the mound over a long time and accumulated to a depth of 1.5 m in places on the slopes of the mound. Several stone-kerbed hearths and layers made up of crumbled animal bones (food refuse) were found, but there were no traces of buildings,

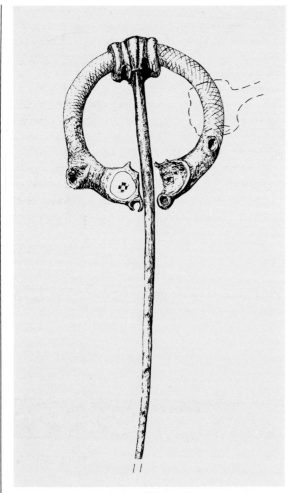

49 Bronze penannular brooch (ring diameter 4 cm) (drawing D Warner).

though it is likely that a number of structures stood on and near the mound.

Many interesting small finds came from different levels of phase 2. These included more than 40 small pieces of local shale on which intricate geometric and interlaced patterns had been scratched (*Fig 50*). These are called trial- or motif-pieces because some were used by craftsmen trying to work out how a complicated pattern should be inscribed correctly, for example on a mould for a bronze object. Some of the circles on the Gransha pieces were set out using a pair of compasses, and one of the iron objects from the same level could well be a leg from such an instrument. Other finds included a long-handled iron spoon, a stylus, a few pieces of clay moulds for casting decorated bronze objects and over 30 polished or rubbed

50 Shale motif-piece from phase 2 (height 4.5 cm).

stones of various sizes and shapes. The unusual number of rubbing stones points to at least one other craft besides metalworking, perhaps to do with the finishing of textiles.

In one area of the uppermost deposits of this phase a series of tiny parallel ridges and grooves, each about 1 cm high and 10 cm wide, was recognized. One possibility is that these strange features are the remains of seed drills, 'frozen' by the sudden dumping of large quantities of make-up when the site was dramatically remodelled in preparation for the final phase of activity.

In phase 2 the summit of the ridge was heightened by only a few centimetres but the middle slopes were raised about a metre by the dumps of occupation and other material. Over a lengthy period this resulted in a slight increase in the size of the domed area at the summit of the mound but there was no sign of a deliberate effort to heighten the mound, increase its summit area or to fortify it.

Phase 3
This began with a large-scale heightening of the mound with a dump of clean gravelly clay. This was about 1 m thick at the centre and 1.6 m at the edges of the platform. The material was probably obtained by trimming off the ends of the ridge on the east and west sides. The result was the creation of the flat-topped mound which survived almost until the time of excavation. This episode probably dates from around the 10th century and it certainly took place before the coming of the Anglo-Normans as the numerous finds from the summit were all of Early Christian period type.

At the east edge of the remodelled mound a small structure of dry masonry was erected (mostly removed in quarrying) but the main evidence for activity was provided by 30 large pits which had been filled up with soil and occupation rubbish. The pits, and the base of the disturbed topsoil between them, produced a number of Early Christian period finds: souterrain ware, iron knives, a 'strike-a-light' and a green and white, herringbone-pattern glass bead, but the most important was a fine, bronze ringed pin. The summit level was too disturbed to show if a substantial dwelling had stood on the mound, but no ordinary rath has produced a comparable series of large pits.

Three important points seem to emerge from the two seasons of quite limited rescue work at Gransha. First, the mound was shown to be entirely of pre-Norman date, and in phase 3 it was raised significantly to gain extra height. A phase of deliberate heightening had been recorded in other Early Christian period mounds, such as Lismahon, Co Down, and clearly the Irish did deliberately raise defended settlement mounds, anticipating, and possibly even influencing, some features of Anglo-Norman mottes. Second, the deposits and finds of phases 1 and 2 were of unusual character, quite unlike the finds from an 'ordinary' excavated rath, and would have been of great interest even if found in isolation at a single-period site. Thirdly, the stratified mound contained a very well-preserved record of the detailed sequence of changing settlements, a reminder that evidence of similar high quality could be expected at other mounds.

CJL

Lynn, C J, 'Excavations at Gransha mound, County Down, 1972 and 1982: interim report', *Ulster J Archaeol* 48 (1985), 81–90.

20. CIVIL ENGINEERING IN THE EARLY CHRISTIAN PERIOD

BIG GLEBE
Co Londonderry

C 760340

This mound was excavated in 1976 before its complete destruction in a farm improvement scheme. It stood on a low ridge, 2.5 km south of the coast at Mussenden, and from its windy summit there was an extensive view in all directions. The mound was large, with a flat top about 20 m in diameter and over 7 m higher than the surrounding pasture. It was surrounded by a ditch with an overall diameter of more than 70 m (*Fig 51*). The monument was described over 140 years ago in the Ordnance Survey Memoir for the parish of Dunboe and several features existed then which had disappeared by 1976. These included a causeway up to the summit, which was surrounded by a stone parapet, with two stone 'gate pillars' at the top of the causeway.

Before excavation the mound was thought to be an Anglo-Norman motte because its appearance and position exactly fitted the standard concept of what a motte should be. Several factors, however, raised some doubts. One was the report of the causeway to the summit and the stone parapet around the top, features more typical of raths or ring-forts. Another was the location of the

51 *Mound at the start of excavation from east.*

mound in an area not known to have been overrun by the Normans in the early stages of the conquest. These initial doubts were justified because excavation showed that the mound had indeed been constructed and its summit occupied in the Early Christian period.

The mound was defended in its earliest phase by a wall of dry-built boulders around the edge of the summit. There was a gap on the south, presumably corresponding with the site of the entrance mentioned in the OS Memoir. At the centre of the slightly domed summit the burnt outline of a wicker house, 7 m in diameter, was uncovered (*Fig 52*). The wall line was marked by 111 stake-holes, 60 cm deep on average. The stake-holes were unusually deep and it is possible that the stakes were driven when the gravelly soil of the new mound had not consolidated. The relatively light wicker structure doubtless needed to be well anchored against the wind in this exposed position. The house had a paved entrance on the east and there were numerous internal stake-holes and pits. Another smaller structure stood to the north. This may have communicated with the main house, but the area of contact was disturbed by recent cultivation. The only finds associated with this first phase were sherds of souterrain ware, pieces of two bronze pins and a quern-stone, but

52 *House plan.*

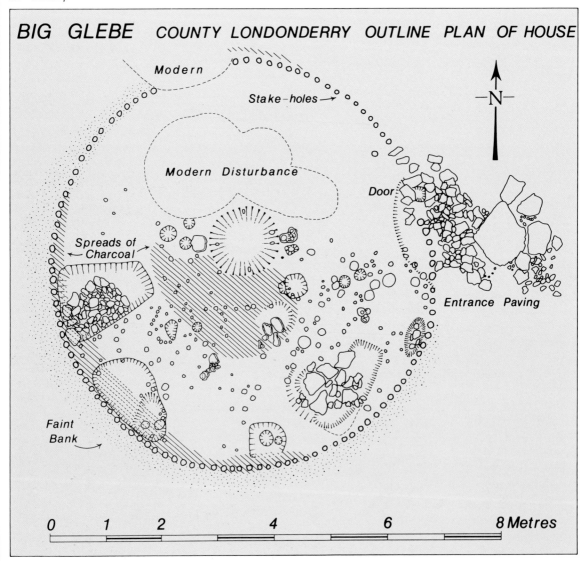

radiocarbon dates from the burnt remains of the main house suggest that it was built in or around the 10th century AD.

After this initial period of occupation the mound was heightened, mainly at the edges, by dumping fresh soil. The primary perimeter wall was used as a revetment for the added material. At the same time a small souterrain was built, curving around the south-west edge of the summit for about 10 m. The surface of the primary occupation level formed its floor and the inner face of the original revetment wall served as its outer wall. The remains of the wicker buildings on the summit were covered by new structures, perhaps of rectangular plan, the lower walls incorporating boulders. The remains of this second and final phase of occupation were badly disturbed by recent cultivation of the summit, but souterrain ware continued in use.

The excavation of these superficial layers showed that the mound had been abandoned for settlement before the end of the Early Christian period. But the possibility remained that further habitation traces lay deeper in the mound and that it had been heightened in several stages, with long or short periods of occupation between. It came as a great surprise, therefore, to discover that the remaining 5 or 6 m of the mound at Big Glebe had been built up in a single operation from the old ground surface. There were no occupation layers deeper in the mound and any doubt that the whole mound (up to the primary summit phase) had been built at one time was dispelled by the discovery on its east side of a large curving ramp, revetted with a wall of boulders on the north side, leading up to the top of a short but massive wall running in an arc at right angles to the ramp (*Fig 53*). The wall was about 3 m high at its top, which was near the centre of the summit of the finished mound.

It seems likely that this ramp, which was more than 2 m wide, was built to allow animals with panniers or carts and sledges to reach the highest part of the mound from the quarry of mound material, which must have been the ditch. From the top of the ramp the soil was perhaps dumped

53 *Revetment of ramp, left; arc of wall, right foreground.*

outwards in all directions, a suggestion supported by the angles of tip-lines in the mound. Mound-building above the internal ramp may have been completed using the summit access causeway on the south-west (the one destroyed in the 19th century). The discovery of this ramp, which at present is unique among excavated sites, proved that the mound had been planned and constructed as a high platform from the start. The only traces of pre-mound activity were a few prehistoric hearths and pits. This suggests that other defended mounds were constructed deliberately in the Early Christian period and that mound growth did not always happen gradually or 'accidentally', in a series of relatively small heightenings, as had been the case at several rath-mounds excavated elsewhere like Gransha, Co Down (p 38).

The discovery of the buried construction ramp underlines the careful planning which went into the building of this impressive landmark, now sadly destroyed. Similar, but less solidly preserved, expedients were doubtless used at other sites. For example rath ditches may have been cut in such a way that material excavated from near the ditch bottom could be carried up a gently sloping path and dumped off the top of the partly constructed bank, using the bank as a 'barrow-run'. This would mean that material for one part of the bank of a substantial rath could have been derived from the ditch at other points on the perimeter.

The person or group who built, and presumably lived on, Big Glebe mound could draw on considerable resources and was surely of high status, yet the house and domestic equipment are no more impressive than those found in many 'ordinary' settlements of the period, some of which have no earthworks at all. The written sources make it clear that wealth in the Early Christian period was measured in terms of cattle, land, personal possessions (many of which were perishable) and numbers of dependent farmers. The evidence from the Big Glebe mound suggests that wealth could be displayed by the erection of impressive earthworks, but that notably larger or more elaborate houses than usual did not necessarily go hand in hand with high status.

CJL

21. ULSTER'S OLDEST WOODEN HOUSES

DEER PARK FARMS, GLENARM
Co Antrim

D 288088

A large mound stood on a north-facing slope at the upper end of Glenarm until late in 1984, when it began to be removed by archaeological excavation before destruction in a farm improvement scheme. The mound was flat-topped, about 25 m in diameter across the summit and 6 m high. It was surrounded by a wide ditch, very deep on the uphill side. It was clear before excavation that this was another complex raised rath, as buried occupation layers could be traced in patches bare of grass on the mound's sides, though it was not evident what archaeological 'riches' lay in store.

The excavation (still in progress at the time of writing) has revealed an amazing sequence of enclosed Early Christian settlements, probably representing continuous occupation from the 6th to the 10th century. The remains of more than 30 circular dwellings, mostly defined by circles of closely-spaced stake-holes, were found at various levels. The surviving evidence shows that a typical house of 6 m diameter would have had about 100 upright stakes in the wall with a gap, 1 m wide and flanked by a pair of large post-holes, marking the site of the door. It appears that three or four buildings, on average, stood at any one time.

Unlike the sequences in the mounds already described, at Gransha (natural hillock, later heightened) and Big Glebe (large built mound, later heightened), the Glenarm mound owes its height and size largely to prolonged occupation

54 *Double-walled wicker round house with encircling paths.*

with the formation of middens and the periodic dumping of clean soil inside a rath. At only one stage was the site heightened significantly, when an average of 1.5 m depth of gravel was added to convert the western area of a rath which had nearly filled up with waterlogged occupation layers into a platform. This gradual build-up at Deer Park Farms, however, surely suggests some intention on the part of the occupants to raise the site: they never attempted to level or remove or properly drain the remains of middens and structures in the site. They always preferred to cover old layers and structures and to start anew on a slightly higher, and often very uneven, surface.

The sequence of major phases and earthwork construction at this site is worth summarizing because it shows for the first time in detail how, and to some extent why, a flat settlement grew into a large mound.

The Early Christian occupation site started as a simple rath enclosure with an earthen bank. This was about 2 m high and in a second phase was faced with a revetment of basalt boulders on the inside. The space enclosed was about 25 m in diameter and occupation material started to build up in it, forming thick organic midden layers, deepest at the downhill side of the enclosure. An unusual inturned entrance passage was added to the original rath entrance on the east side. At the inner end of this a double-walled wicker round house, 7 m in diameter, was constructed (*Fig 54*). The walls of the house were formed of hazel rods, tightly woven in a complex spiralling pattern around stouter uprights, and they survived to a maximum height of 60 cm (2 ft). The space between the walls was packed with soft organic material, probably a mixture of straw, moss and heather, an early form of 'cavity walling'. Evidence for bedding areas and internal screens was found inside the house, and near the wall on the north side a small brooch dating to about AD 800 was found in bedding material (*Fig 56*). These are the first preserved wattle walls to have been found in a rath excavation. They owed their survival to the waterlogging of the lower layers of the mound and the fact that the house was encased in a thick dump of gravel build-up before it had decayed. At this level and below, wooden staves and leather shoes,

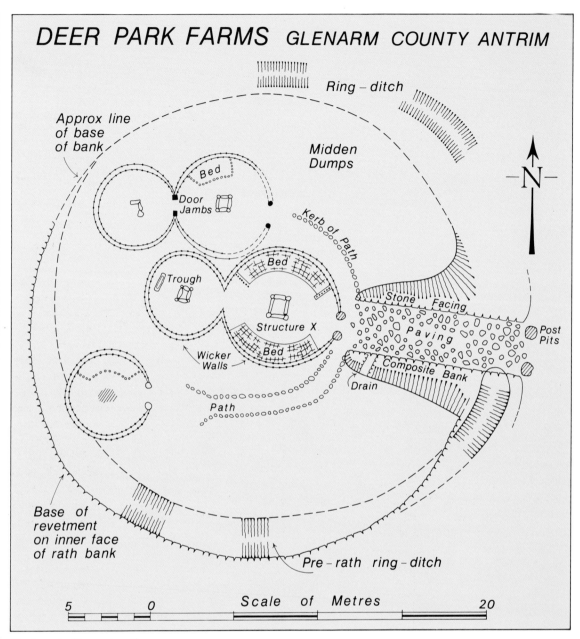

DEER PARK FARMS GLENARM COUNTY ANTRIM

Ring – ditch

Midden Dumps

Approx line of base of bank

Bed

Door Jambs

Kerb of Path

- N -

Trough

Bed

Structure X

Stone Facing

Paving

Post Pits

Wicker Walls

Bed

Composite Bank

Drain

Path

Base of revetment on inner face of rath bank

Pre - rath ring - ditch

Scale of Metres

5   0   20

55 Layout of houses in rath.

objects not normally preserved in raths, were found in the damp organic midden layers. In 1987 the remains of four further houses with preserved wattle walls were found at the same level in the rath (*Fig 55*).

Dumps of gravel and clay up to 1.5 m thick were added to the site in several stages and a low mound was created, using the primary rath bank as an external revetment. A slight bank was added to the perimeter of this low platform and this too was neatly stone-faced on the inside, with a gap on the east to provide access to the summit by a high-level ramp along the axis of the earlier, now buried, rath entrance. The remains of more than twenty circular structures, 5 to 8 m in diameter, were found at various levels in the occupation

56 Bronze brooch-pin, glass beads and stud.

57 Revetment walls of ditch and mound.

deposits which built up on the platform. Where clear evidence survived for the walls of these buildings it was also for wicker construction: they were delimited by circles of stake-holes, sometimes, if the structure burnt down, with ribbons of charcoal clearly showing the horizontal wattles woven in and out through the stakes. At this high level no unburnt organic materials survived so the numerous occupation layers were very thin. Souterrain ware was used in this lengthy phase, which also produced about 50 coloured glass beads (Fig 56), mostly broken, and iron objects such as knives, a billhook and shears.

In the penultimate phase of occupation the entrance ramp was heightened and a massive revetment wall was added to the outside of the mound. This was best represented on the uphill side (Fig 57), where it sloped upwards from a neat shelf in the inner edge of the ditch to a height of a least 3 m. This gave the mound the impressive external appearance of a large cashel and suggests that its occupants must have been important to have been able to call on the labour for such an undertaking.

This phase must have spanned several generations, but eventually the inhabitants decided to raise their occupation surface (for the last time) by dumping fresh subsoil on the mound, up to a maximum of 1.8 m on the south and east. On the east a T-plan souterrain was built at the upper edge of the mound in step with this build-up, explaining why the dump was thickest at this side. A second souterrain was constructed at about the same time in a curving trench on the north side of the mound. Occupation continued in the Early Christian period (shown by finds of some 700 sherds of souterrain ware in the topsoil) and the site was eventually abandoned, but it is impossible to suggest when, as all traces of layers and above-ground structures of the final phase of the settlement had been destroyed by later cultivation of the mound summit.

While the loss of this important landmark and archaeological resource has to be regretted, we must admit that its excavation has provided evidence of unique quality for the layout of a series of superimposed Early Christian settlements. Even by normal standards the remains of structures and layers high in the mound were very well preserved and the evidence was unusually clear-cut. But the waterlogging of occupation layers near its base, unique for a 'dry-land' site, has preserved the remains of buildings and organic midden layers, with enormous quantities of environmental evidence, so well that at this level, deep in the mound, you could imagine that the site had been abandoned for less than a decade, rather than a thousand years.

CJL

RATHMULLAN
Co Down

J 478373
Scheduled

Rathmullan, which gave its name to the townland on the south coast of the Lecale peninsula, was yet another mound drawn to the attention of HMBB – this time threatened with removal in 1978 because of its proximity to a modern house. Although the mound was small (6 m high, its summit 11 m across) compared with those already described, its ridge-top location made Rathmullan a well-known landmark overlooking the shore at Minerstown (*Fig 58*).

Before excavation the monument was believed to be a motte, an Anglo-Norman castle mound, like several in east Down, including Clough (in State care), 6 km to the south. This was because of its appearance and the fact that a late medieval tower-house, a type of small castle, once stood a short distance to the north. The excavation proved that Rathmullan had certainly been heightened by the Anglo-Normans, presumably for use as a motte, early in the medieval period. But underneath the medieval deposits was a substantial and long-occupied Early Christian raised rath or rath-mound.

The Anglo-Norman layers were excavated and removed down to the top of the Early Christian platform, at which stage excavation ceased in all but one quadrant and the monument was consolidated. This operation reduced the nuisance posed by the mound (through slippage and poor ventilation) and 'put the clock back' to the extent

that the surviving mound can now be described as the remnant of an Early Christian rath, as opposed to a Norman motte. Deposits in the mound, therefore, bridged the junction between the Early Christian and medieval periods. This is an important transition, because the Norman conquest of 1177 brought the Early Christian period firmly to an end and introduced a new range of material (particularly pottery), building methods and craft techniques. Culture and society rapidly changed over much of Ireland, particularly in areas settled by Anglo-Norman families. In Ulster, pre-existing Irish fortifications, some of which had been abandoned for generations, were frequently taken over and adapted by the first Norman settlers, and several of these sites have been chosen in the past for research excavation in the hope of tracing interaction between the native and Norman populations.

The Early Christian levels at Rathmullan were excavated in a fairly small area but amounted to a total thickness of about 2 m. The outlines of parts of four superimposed buildings were exposed – two round wooden houses at the bottom and rectilinear structures with stone and earth footings above (*Fig 59*). A small souterrain with galleries on two levels was probably connected to one of the later rectangular houses, but the weight of the motte had dangerously split most of its massive lintels.

The medieval levels were even more interesting. A few sherds of wheel-thrown pottery, of types probably made in France and England, were found *under* the motte in the surface of the rath. Similar pottery was found on the motte, so it seems possible that this pottery was used briefly on the site by the Normans before they got round to heightening the rath. We could not be certain that the rath had been abandoned before this time, but it is unlikely that this pottery would have been imported by pre-Norman rath dwellers.

No traces of perimeter defences were found, like a palisade, or wall, or archers' pits, often present on fortified mounds. But the entrance to

58 Mound before excavation from south-east.

PHASES

7   RUBBISH PITS

6

                                    STONE FOOTINGS

5

                                    STONE SCATTER

4

                               SOUTERRAIN AND
                               HOUSE

3

                               STAKE-HOLE
                               HOUSE

2

                               GULLIES.
                               POST-HOLES

1

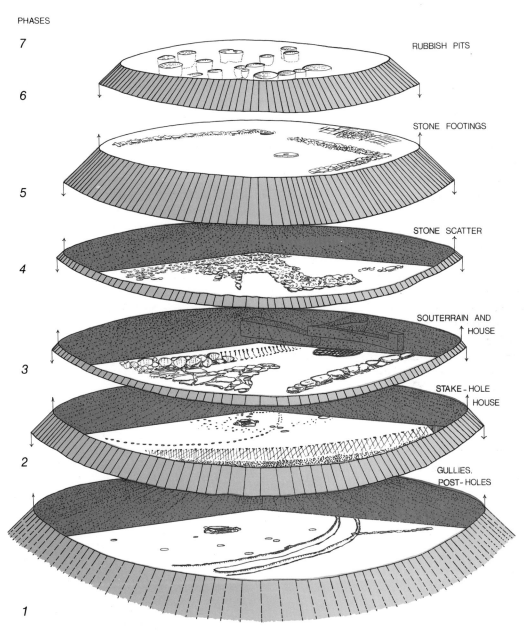

59   *Diagram of structural phases.*

49

the primary motte summit led through a stone-lined gate passage sunk into the upper edge of the mound on the south. On the mound summit were the burnt remains of a small building with associated occupation layers. The structure, 9 m by more than 6 m (the east side had eroded away), was indicated by a rectilinear outline of loose stones, charcoal spreads and twisted iron nails.

While the mound-top location was clearly selected for defensive purposes, the Norman settlement on Rathmullan seems to have been purely domestic and the excavation revealed no features or finds of military significance. Mottes are sometimes described as earth bases for timber archery towers, and there is a well-known illustration of such a motte-castle in the Bayeux Tapestry, but several excavated examples in Ulster appear to have served a dual function as stronghold and residence. Motte summits generally seem to have been abandoned by the Norman colonists as soon as it became safe to move down to more convenient accommodation on level ground.

An interesting range of medieval pottery came from the primary occupation level on the motte, including jugs from Bristol and western France, and a few sherds of native coarse souterrain ware. There was enough of the latter to suggest that it might have remained in use locally as cooking pottery in the early years after the invasion. Some quantities of English-style pottery products from a medieval kiln discovered in Downpatrick in the 1960s were also recovered. Two millstones, about 1 m in diameter, were re-used in the structure, one

in the wall-footings, the other as a hearth. Small finds included tiny gilded bronze buckles, bronze tweezers, a bone gaming-piece and several coins, one of John de Courcy, the Norman conqueror of Ulster, minted in Downpatrick in about 1195, and two pennies of Henry II (one a forgery of silver foil on copper). These layers were covered by a dump of clean soil 1 m thick and, although some sherds of Downpatrick pottery were scattered about, there was no further occupation on the mound, which was perhaps maintained for a while for use in an emergency.

The dating evidence suggests that the primary occupation on the summit took place in about 1200. This is perhaps the most interesting outcome of the excavation because it suggests that the period of currency of several of the pottery types present at Rathmullan may have begun several decades earlier than had been realized. This is important because the date-ranges of contexts at many excavated sites in Britain and Ireland have to be worked out only on the basis of such pottery finds. Coins of rare, short-lived, types like those of John de Courcy are seldom found in contexts so secure as Rathmullan, and in Ulster we have the advantage of knowing that virtually all of this material must post-date the year of his invasion, 1177.

CJL

Lynn, C J, 'The excavation of Rathmullan, a raised rath and motte in County Down', *Ulster J Archaeol* 44 & 45 (1981–2), 61–171.

23. SAINTS, SCHOLARS AND SMITHS

MOVILLA ABBEY
Co Down

J 504744

The last standing remains of St Malachy's late 12th-century Augustinian foundation at Movilla are the ruins of its mainly 13th-century church, standing on the hill above Newtownards. Several medieval sandstone grave-covers have also been discovered and are now set in the walls of the

church. Only one grave slab survives above ground from the great foundation of St Finnian, who died in AD 579. Movilla, as a centre of scholarship and craftsmanship, survived at least one Viking raid, in 825, and probably remained active until the changes of the 12th century.

The greater part of both the pre-Norman and medieval monasteries lies beneath a large municipal cemetery, a road and a housing estate, so much of the archaeology is lost for all time. Therefore when perhaps the last untouched part of the site was threatened by a re-alignment of Movilla Road, a series of excavations was organized to try to fill out the rather sketchy history of this once-important religious house.

The excavations in 1980 and 1981 revealed evidence of a very long and intensive occupation of the site, and of a variety of crafts and industries that were carried on there. Finds of flint tools demonstrate that some use was made of the area in prehistoric times, but it was not until the Early Christian period that there was any substantial settlement. The density of this early occupation is shown by the pieces of coarse, hand-made pottery that were found scattered about in their thousands, as well as other everyday objects such as quern-stones. Traces of timber structures, built and rebuilt many times, were also uncovered.

Without doubt the most important finds from the early monastery were those illustrating the skills of the craftsmen, who worked in iron, bronze and glass. There was much industrial debris: lumps of slag, broken pieces of crucible and fragments of scrap metal, all informative but perhaps not very exciting. But a few objects do stimulate the imagination, for example a trial-piece, on which the bronze-smith rehearsed his designs of triangles, scrolls and arcs, and a glass-headed pin, decorated with discs and trails of different coloured glass. The technical and artistic sophistication of such objects is certainly at variance with the impression of material poverty given by the simple timber houses and rather crude pottery.

Little seems to have changed until the 13th century, when a substantial building was erected, of which the stone foundations and some of the stone-paved floor survived (*Fig 60*). The size and strength of these walls suggest that the building probably had an upper story and was occupied by someone of consequence. The walls were about 1.2 m thick, and the building was about 8 m wide and at least as long. Within and around it many fragments of good quality, wheel-made and glazed pottery were found; some were locally made but

60   West end of 13th-century stone building.

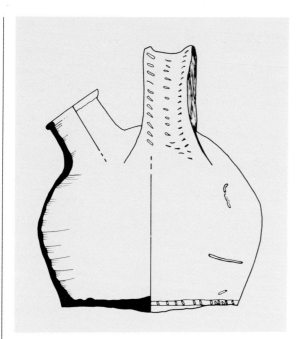

61 *Fourteenth-century pottery urinal* (drawing *R Ivens*).

others were imported, perhaps from as far away as France. The most striking and unusual pot was the badly fragmented but almost complete remains of a 14th-century urinal, the only one of its type ever found in Ireland, and almost certainly imported (*Fig 61*).

In the later 14th century this area fell into decay. Finds of painted window glass and lead strips suggest that the neighbouring church was also in a state of decay. Perhaps this is why it was partly rebuilt in the 15th century?

The excavation of a very small part of what was once an extensive monastic settlement has thus given some tantalising glimpses of a long and varied occupation, as well as an insight into the skills of the Early Christian craftsmen.

RJI

Ivens, R J, 'Movilla Abbey, Newtownards, Co Down: excavations 1981', *Ulster J Archaeol* 47 (1984), 71–108.
Yates, M J, 'Preliminary excavations at Movilla Abbey, Co Down, 1980', *Ulster J Archaeol* 46 (1983), 53–66.

24. WHY DIG AT A SITE IN STATE CARE?

DEVENISH
Co Fermanagh

H 224469

State care

Excavation is sometimes done in connection with conservation work on sites in State care. This may be designed to investigate problems which it is important to understand before undertaking con-solidation, like the sagging wall at St John's Point (*p 29*), or it may be done to increase our under-standing of the site's development and to clarify the remains for the visitor. Devenish provides a good example of this kind of excavation.

Devenish is a well-known and important monastic island in Lower Lough Erne and it has been in the care of the State since the Disestablish-ment of the Church of Ireland in 1869 (*Fig 62*). The visible remains are impressive in their beautiful lakeland setting, but the ruins span the period only from the 12th to the early 17th centuries. Much of the long history of the site, from the time of its founder, St Molaise, in the 6th century, lies buried.

Whenever the ground has to be disturbed, there-fore, an archaeologist is at hand to investigate and record any ancient features which may be revealed. There is a peculiar irregularity in the fence-line north of the 12th-century round tower because in the winter of 1972–3, when holes were being dug for a new fence, mortared stones were found and investigated. They turned out to be the greatly ruined foundations of a second round tower, and these are now laid out for the visitor to see (*Fig 63*).

At the highest point of the site is St Mary's Augustinian Priory, with substantial remains of a 15th-century church, bell-tower and cloister. Earl-ier conservation work on the east range of the cloister had created certain problems, and in 1972 it was decided to excavate the fragmentary east range to resolve these inherited problems and

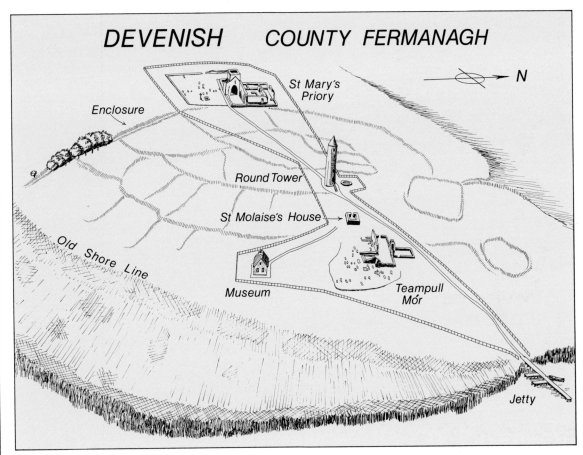

DEVENISH   COUNTY FERMANAGH

N

Enclosure

St Mary's
Priory

Round Tower

St Molaise's House →

Old Shore Line

Museum

Teampull
Mór

Jetty

62   Bird's-eye view diagram.

reveal the full plan for the visitor. The work was done by D M Waterman between 1972 and 1974, and his plan shows just how complicated the archaeology was (*Fig 64*).

The east range in its final form overlay an unfinished earlier range, and both overlay a yet

63   Foundation of excavated round tower with 12th-century tower beyond.

earlier building. Below these was a series of infilled ditches, and there was a scatter of pits and post-holes over the whole area. The finds indicated a 15th-century date for the walls, but unfortunately there was no dating evidence for the ditches. In the standing remains there are signs of intense burning, and excavation produced a thick layer of burnt wood, clay, straw, twigs, nails and grains of wheat and oats in the northern end of the east range, evidence for a fierce fire in the late 15th or early 16th century. Sherds of fine late medieval pottery from France, Germany, Spain and the Netherlands could be explained by the known importance of Lough Erne as a route for international pilgrims to St Patrick's Purgatory in Lough Derg, Co Donegal. Churches on the islands and shores of the lough provided hospitality for the travellers.

The finding of the buried ditch under the east range of St Mary's was interesting but also frustrating because it could not be dated. South-east of St Mary's is a still-visible earthwork, with a bank and

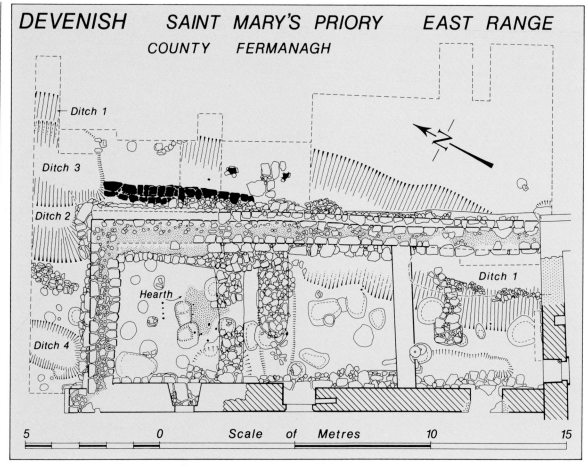

DEVENISH   SAINT MARY'S PRIORY   EAST RANGE
COUNTY FERMANAGH

Ditch 1

Ditch 3

Ditch 2

Hearth

Ditch 4

Ditch 1

5   0   Scale   of   Metres   10   15

64   Dudley Waterman's excavation plan.

uphill ditch, which could line up with the St Mary's ditch. A small trench was therefore opened across the visible remains, but again no evidence of date was found. The excavator was cautious in interpreting this feature, but as all the surviving structures and earthworks lie within it (downslope), except for St Mary's (*Fig 62*), it is very tempting to see it as the early monastic boundary. This remains our working hypothesis until further work is possible.

AH

Hamlin, A, 'Some further documentary evidence for the round tower at Devenish, County Fermanagh', *Ulster J Archaeol* 39 (1976), 73–74.

Radford, C A R, 'Devenish', *Ulster J Archaeol* 33 (1970), 55–62.

Waterman, D M, 'A second round tower at Devenish, Co Fermanagh', *Ulster J Archaeol* 36 & 37 (1973–4), 100–102.

Waterman, D M, 'St Mary's Priory, Devenish: excavation of the east range, 1972–4', *Ulster J Archaeol* 42 (1979), 34–50.

TULLYLISH
Co Down

J 084484

The small village of Tullylish lies in the heartland of the once-thriving linen industry of the Bann Valley. Near the present Church of Ireland church is the ruined 'Black Tower' of a late 18th-century church. This tower stands on a low mound, some 50 m in diameter, still in use as a graveyard, which until recently had been taken to be the extent of the Early Christian monastery. The Annals of Ulster point to a community here as early as AD 809, when Dúnchú, abbot of Tullylish (*Telach-liss*), was killed beside the shrine of St Patrick, in the abbot's house of *Telach-liss*. Later medieval records refer to a parish church at Tullylish.

Because of these documented associations HMBB arranged to observe the site during prelim-

65 Inner ditch.

inary clearance for a church hall in a neighbouring field in 1983. It quickly became clear that there were major archaeological remains in this area, and the Church of Ireland authorities readily agreed to an excavation during a lull in the building.

During the building work large quantities of medieval pottery came from what was suspected to be the topmost fill of a ditch. Archaeological excavation proved this to be the case and a large, steep-sided, flat-bottomed and rock-cut ditch was revealed, some 4.6 m wide and 2.8 m deep, about 30 m outside the graveyard boundary. Immediately inside the ditch were traces of a large earthen rampart some 5 m wide, and inside this was a broad shallow ditch, about 1.5 m deep. In the bottom of this ditch were remains indicating that it had been used for a variety of craft and domestic activities, including metalworking. The area between the ditch and the present graveyard was occupied by the very slight remains of an ancient cemetery.

However, this was not the end of the story. Below the bottom layer of the shallow ditch more archaeological remains were found, and eventually another ditch was revealed, even wider and deeper than the first. This ditch was about 5 m wide and 3.6 m deep, but because it was cut into the hillside, the bottom of the ditch was about 5 m below the surface of the enclosed area – a formidable obstacle (*Fig 65*).

Radiocarbon measurements indicate that this massive ditch was already in use by the 7th century, and was probably dug a century or so earlier. In the 9th century it had filled up, and a new ditch (the outer one) was dug to replace it. The shallow depression which was all that remained of the first ditch was used as a sheltered working area.

Gradually the outer ditch silted up, and the pottery and other objects found in the fill indicate that it was finally abandoned in about 1400. At about the same time a large corn-drying kiln was built. This consisted of a shaft, 2 m in diameter, cut into the ground, lined with a stone wall, and three

66 *Corn-drying kiln.*

67 *Part of hand-made decorated pot (height 8 cm).*

stone-lined flues (*Fig 66*). In one of these flues, according to wind direction, a fire would be lit and the draught of hot air used to dry corn. It is not clear exactly what the nature of the medieval occupation was, but one possibility is that this was the site of the parish church, and that the parish priest farmed and received corn as tithe payments.

Amongst the many finds were several silver pennies of Edward II and III, and these were especially valuable in helping to date both the final phases of the ditch fill and the associated pottery. Large amounts of this very skilfully hand-made and highly decorated pottery were found in the upper fill of the outer ditch (*Fig 67*). Other finds included a small medieval bronze brooch, and a range of the lignite rings or bangles which are commonly found on Early Christian period sites. Many of the Tullylish examples were unfinished and they were obviously being made at the site.

The excavations at Tullylish have revealed exactly what the place-name suggested should be there, a hillock (*tulach*) with an enclosure or enclosed area on it (*lios*). It may be that the name derives from the monastic enclosure, but the excavated evidence allows two rather different interpretations. Both ditches could relate to the monastic occupation, or the older, inner, ditch could belong to an earlier, pre-Christian settlement. More excavation would be needed to investigate this point, but the 1983 excavations were richly rewarding, despite the rescue circumstances.

RJI

ARMAGH   H 879451

It would be possible to devote a whole book to defining a city and discussing urban origins, but if any Irish town deserves the title of this chapter it is Armagh. In the years since 1975 several small-scale rescue and salvage excavations have been done in the city, mostly on sites being redeveloped because of bombing.

Any account of a subject as complex as the growth of a historic town in and around important ecclesiastical sites can only be selective. But it is important to recognize the contribution that excavation can make when, as at Armagh, so little survives above ground. Most of what we know about its history and topographical development in the Early Christian and medieval periods comes from written sources. No masonry earlier than the 13th century survives, and the only medieval buildings of which parts remain above ground are

the friary and cathedral. The annals contain many references to ecclesiastical buildings from about AD 800 onwards but there is little evidence for earlier developments. We have only 7th-century and later traditions about St Patrick and claims that Armagh, as an important ecclesiastical and later monastic centre, dates back to the 5th century. Still more difficult to prove are suggestions that the modern circular street pattern follows the lines of pre-Christian earthworks enclosing the hilltop, either for a secular stronghold or ritual site (*Fig 68*). It certainly seems unlikely that the siting of what became Ireland's premier Christian site at Armagh was unrelated to the important pre-Christian ceremonial site at Navan, *Emain Macha*, 3 km to the west, but the relationship between the sites is obscure. It is possible that Armagh was founded on a hill close to Navan in order to maintain the

68   Air view of Armagh with Scotch Street at bottom left.

tradition and prestige of religious worship in the area. Whatever the truth of the early traditions, by the 8th century Armagh had certainly become established as the paramount ecclesiastical centre in Ireland on the simple assertion that St Patrick was the apostle of the Irish and that he himself had designated Armagh – 'the place he loved more than any other' – as his chief centre.

The earliest Christian churches in Ireland were built of wood. The first record of a stone church in the annals is to one at Armagh in 789, but this was unusual, and timber was certainly used for ecclesiastical buildings long after this date and throughout the Early Christian period for domestic structures. Several churches, probably very small by modern standards, stood on the hill at Armagh in the Early Christian period as well as an abbot's house, library, kitchen and of course dwellings. Later in the period there was at least one round tower of masonry. Most of these structures stood within a hilltop enclosure (the 'rath') with an entrance on the east near which stood a high cross (one of several). It has been suggested that the curve of Castle Street corresponds to the line of the rath, but a substantial early ditch on a different line was found near here in excavations in 1967. Given the long period of time involved, however, it is likely that the hill was enclosed in a series of earthworks, any one, or several, of which could have been the historic 'rath'.

In 1126 a large abbey of Augustinian Canons, dedicated to SS Peter and Paul, was founded in the Abbey Street area and survived to the end of the 16th century. In the 1260s the present cathedral was built and its construction must have swept away traces of several earlier buildings. In the same decade another Continental order was brought to Armagh when a Franciscan friary (ruins in State care) was built to the south-east of the hill. Outside the rath the city was divided into three districts or *trians*, but it is not known if their boundaries were physically defined on the ground, if they occupied all of the lower slopes of the hill, and if they were completely built over with ecclesiastical buildings or the houses of monks or tradespeople. We have further documentary evidence for the late medieval topography of Armagh from 17th-century inquisitions (statistical inquiries) and from a picture map of Armagh made in about 1600, probably by the gifted Elizabethan map-maker Richard Bartlett (*Fig 69*).

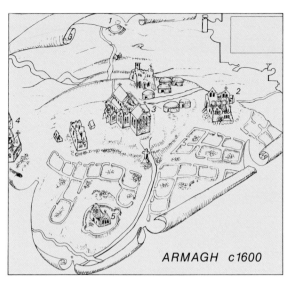

69 *Sketch copy of Bartlett's picture map of Armagh.*
1 Navan Fort.   2 Abbey of SS Peter and
Paul.   3 Cathedral.   4 Friary.   5 Church of Na Ferta.

Against this background, it is clear that Armagh can be regarded as a vast archaeological site, and that any secure excavated evidence from the city will contribute to the picture of its long development. Even 'negative evidence' is important: a lack of features needs to be explained.

The excavations in Armagh since 1975 have mainly concentrated on a number of small sites on either side of Scotch Street (*Fig 70*) which crosses an ancient district, outside the main ecclesiastical nucleus, known as *Na Ferta* (the graves or grave-mounds). It was here, according to the earliest traditions, that St Patrick established his first settlement, only later being given the hilltop by the local chieftain, Dáire. The site was used as a cemetery and a church was in existence by 1090 when 'the stone church of *Na Ferta* was burned and a hundred houses thereround'. By the 13th century a small convent of nuns had been established and this survived until the middle of the 16th century. The intact walls of a small church are shown on Bartlett's *c* 1600 map (*Fig 69*) with ruins of other buildings, perhaps the domestic accommodation, a little further to the west. The last remnants of the church may have been removed in the construction of no. 16 Scotch Street in 1812. The street rises steeply at first from the east but then levels out on a knoll and dips slightly before meeting the incline of the main hill at Market Street. The excavations

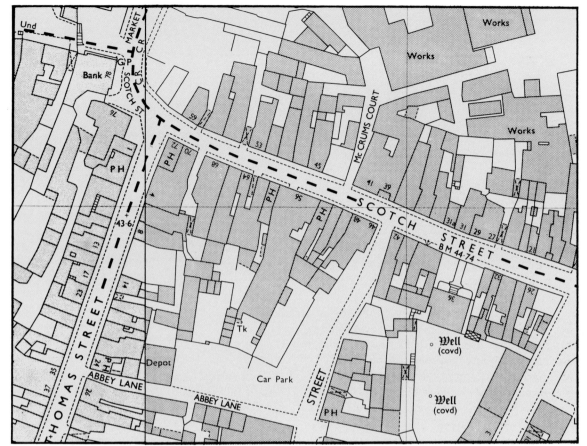

70 *Map of Scotch Street area (scale 1:1550) (from OS 1:1250 Plans 218-6 SW and 218-6 SE, reproduced with the sanction of the Controller of HMSO, Crown Copyright, permit no 165).*

have covered a substantial area of the knoll as a result of a series of small investigations carried out over a 10-year period.

The earliest activity found on the site dated from the Neolithic period (*p 8*). Those remains tend to support, but do not prove, the suggestion that there were some visible prehistoric monuments on the knoll at the start of the Christian era. Such monuments, possibly grave-mounds, may have given the area an aura of sanctity in the minds of the local people and may have provided an appropriate ritual focus for a very early ecclesiastical settlement here.

The earliest feature of the Christian period was uncovered at the highest point of the knoll under no. 48 Scotch Street: a small charcoal- and ash-filled pit which produced a radiocarbon date centring on the 5th century AD. The pit was earlier than a nearby grave and is the only, but surely significant, evidence for activity at the site in the

'Patrician period'. Some time later very shallow burials started. These do not appear to have been surrounded by an enclosure but occurred in clumps and irregular rows and the graves may have been dug over a lengthy period. Burials which seem to relate to this early cemetery were found in no. 43, in the south half of nos 39–41, in nos 46–56 and sporadically at the rear of no. 16. No burials were found further south in the back garden of no. 46 suggesting that the cemetery may have been elongated east–west along the line of what is now Scotch Street. Although little bone survived, one grave in no. 48 contained disarticulated remains of a skull and longbones and appeared to have been marked by a pair of wooden uprights at the west end. Several intact burials were contained in what seemed to be traces of oak log coffins. Radiocarbon dates suggest that the timber for one coffin in no. 48 had been growing in or around the 6th century. This confirmed the

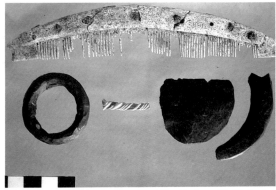

71 *Bone comb, glass rod and cut lignite from 50–56 Scotch Street.*

72 *Stone-lined medieval well.*

antiquity of the burials and suggests that they do in fact constitute the 'cemetery of the martyrs' said by Muirchú in his 7th-century life of the saint to occupy the site first used by Patrick in Armagh.

Although later graves were dug from time to time, the area generally was given over to occupation, chiefly characterized by the remains of craft industries contained in a loamy layer. This was particularly well developed over nos 50–56 Scotch Street, where the slope of the knoll fell away to the south-west. This phase of industrial activity was indicated by hundreds of tiny chips of amber, waste from the manufacture of glass beads, crucible fragments for bronze-melting, sawn antler (suggesting comb-making) and hundreds of pieces of cut lignite from the manufacture of armlets, finished and partly finished examples of which were found (*Fig 71*). This activity probably dates from around the 10th century.

Where this deposit was thickest in nos 50–56 many post-holes, gullies, stake-holes and pits were cut into the layer. Although no definite outlines of buildings were identified it is certain that the excavated area at least lay adjacent to an Early Christian occupation site. On the south side of the knoll these features were covered by a further layer which had accumulated towards the end of the Early Christian period. This produced a number of fine decorated stick-pins and other evidence for occupation, including pieces of rubble and mortar showing that a masonry structure had been built in the vicinity before the end of the period.

In the back garden of no. 16 two shallow, truncated, stone-lined, wells of rectangular plan were found in 1976 (*Fig 70*). The southern example had silted up gradually and deposits in it may bridge the Early Christian and medieval periods (*Fig 72*). A stick-pin found in its bottom is of 12th-century type, but some medieval material came from higher levels. In the lower fill was a fragment of a Greek porphyry tile (one of three fragments of exotic porphyry from the Scotch Street excavations). This presumably came to Armagh either as a souvenir from some important Continental shrine or was imported as a cover for a relic cavity in an altar. The other well was apparently open at the end of the medieval period. It was filled with mortared masonry rubble and occasional human bones, and a 16th-century coin was found near the top of the fill. The discovery of the wells, and in particular their contents, indicate the presence nearby of a medieval religious house and confirm the evidence of Bartlett's map and local tradition that the medieval church of *Na Ferta* stood on the site of no. 16 Scotch Street, immediately north of the excavated area.

In 1984 the foundations of a masonry building of medieval date, measuring 7 m wide by more than 8 m long, were in fact found during excavations in no. 50 Scotch Street overlying Early Christian deposits. Nearby rubbish pits and occupation layers suggest that this building was used for domestic purposes, but one of the pits produced a small jet cross, clearly of religious significance. The north-west by south-east alignment of the building corresponds with that of ruins shown on Bartlett's map, and it seems likely that they are one and the same, perhaps the remains of the domestic range of the small medieval convent.

After a period of destruction and neglect in the later 16th and 17th centuries, the market town of Armagh expanded in the 18th century and this area was covered by the newly laid-out Scotch Street. The filling of a well at the back of 18th-century premises on no. 56 produced a large number of interesting finds, including a pewter tankard and seven broken but complete 'brown ware' jugs.

One other interesting site in the area was excavated, just round the corner in Market Street. A long east–west trial-trench was excavated through a depth of more than 3 m of organic deposits which had probably built up in a shallow lake over the long period from the 13th to the 17th century. The deposits contained small amounts of pottery, fragments of hurdling, animal bones (including a complete cow skeleton) and a fragment of an octagonal sandstone shaft, perhaps from a cloister arcade. This swamp or lake could have been formed accidentally, perhaps as a result of rubbish blocking a stream, but it could have been a deliberate creation, perhaps for a mill- or fish-pond. The discovery of an underlying spring reminds us of a passage in the Book of the Angel, a 7th-century text in the Book of Armagh, in which it is reported that 'St Patrick was baptizing persons at the spring which is hard by the eastern side of the city . . .'. The lake did not exist in the 7th century but the underlying spring presumably gave rise to a small stream which would have flowed along the line of Thomas Street. In the 7th century this spot could well have been described as close to the east side of the city.

This outline of the ten years of excavations in the Scotch Street area shows how complex the evidence can be from one part of a long-occupied ecclesiastical site. The excavations have been valuable in complementing and supplementing the evidence of written sources. The picture is of pre-historic activity, transient very *early* Early Christian period activity pre-dating a series of early burials, occupation, industrial activity and masonry building before the end of the Early Christian period, a medieval religious house and continuing occupation to the end of the 16th century, a period of demolition and dereliction and finally the growth of the modern town in the 18th century. It is well worth emphasizing that the graves found in Scotch Street are the earliest ecclesiastical remains to have been found in Armagh. The 7th-century belief that this *Na Ferta* area was the earliest Christian site was strong, and the excavations have produced material evidence to support the tradition. Given the pre-eminent position of Armagh in church history and the unique historical importance of its traditional founder this is significant new evidence which would have been lost for ever if the excavations had not taken place when they did.

CJL
JAMcD

Gaskell Brown, C, and Harper, A, 'Excavations on Cathedral Hill, Armagh, 1968', *Ulster J Archaeol* 47 (1984), 109–161.
Reeves, W, *The Ancient Churches of Armagh* (Lusk, 1860).

27. LIFE AND DEATH AT AN EARLY MONASTERY

CATHEDRAL HILL, DOWNPATRICK
Co Down

J 483444
Scheduled

Archaeologists working within a rescue policy sometimes have to make difficult choices. Such was the case on Downpatrick's Cathedral Hill when the church authorities, seeking to expand the cathedral graveyard, sought advice on what part of this historic hill would be least damaged by years of burial (*Fig 73*).

Down Cathedral, on the summit of the hill, is all that survives of a Benedictine monastery founded in the late 12th century. The site (what-

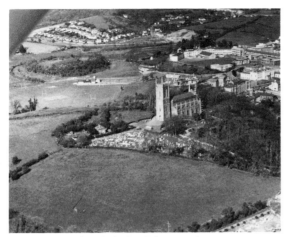

73 *Air view of Cathedral Hill from south-west.*

ever the truth of its association wth St Patrick) is also recognized as having been an Early Christian monastic centre. Excavations in the 1950s, on the western side of the hilltop, revealed extensive traces of Bronze Age occupation, while on the opposite side of the hill excavation had exposed one of only two medieval pottery kilns known in Ireland (*see also p 64*).

Clearly, recommending a site for a new graveyard was not an easy task, for disturbance of the ground almost anywhere on Cathedral Hill could have archaeological implications. It was agreed that the apparently least 'sensitive' area, which would also permit a natural extension to the existing graveyard, was the south-west slope of the hill. This was over 100 m away from the cathedral and outside an earthwork bank, often referred to as 'the hill-fort', which ringed the crest of the hill.

Nevertheless, some excavation was necessary, and in 1985 a long sampling trench on the slope opened the programme. But, contrary to expectations, even at this distance from the supposed nucleus of settlement – the cathedral area – there were rich discoveries to be made, and during the next two summers the excavations were expanded over a large area.

Much of the downslope half of the excavated site was covered with a thick layer of stone rubble and mortar fragments which also filled irregularly-cut trenches. While at first perplexing as an archaeological feature, it soon became clear that here was a 'robbed' building, a large masonry structure quarried for its stone. That the building

was medieval was clear from fragments of glazed tiles which had crested its roof, dressed stones and other artifacts found in the rubble. The date of the 'robbing' was provided by a few pieces of broken wine bottles and clay tobacco pipes discarded by the labourers who had quarried the building in the mid 18th century. The building may indeed have been one of the 'stone cells' discovered on Cathedral Hill and described in a 1744 survey of Co Down. It may also have provided stone for the 18th-century restoration of the cathedral.

The long axis of the building was aligned east–west. The discovery of dressed sandstone quoins and mouldings (some carved with scallop shells, crosses and graffiti faces) and hand-painted window glass suggests that the building had an ecclesiastical purpose, hardly a surprising interpretation with a Benedictine foundation nearby. Unfortunately, however, the 18th-century quarrying had been so extensive that the excavators were unable to prove that it had been a church.

Further upslope the western edge of a medieval cemetery was located, the main concentration of burials probably lying to the east under the present graveyard. Over a dozen shallow inhumations, of adults of both sexes, were found. It appeared that these simple Christian burials were unmarked, for early graves had been cut and disturbed by later ones. Groups of re-buried skulls and longbones showed that some attempts had been made to make good the disturbance to earlier burials.

Beneath the medieval levels excavation found that the site had also served as an Early Christian period cemetery (*Fig 74*), but of the seventeen well-preserved inhumations found, only in one instance did one grave cut another. Perhaps the graves were marked (although how is not known) or the cemetery was less intensively used. Pathological examination, as is often the case, failed to identify any causes of death, but did reveal a variety of diseases and dietary deficiencies, while dental patterns suggested that a number of the dead were related. In one instance the skull of a young woman, who died in her 30s, showed evidence of a violent blow with a sharp tool or weapon, sufficient to fracture it. However, the skull had healed and the blow was not the cause of death. The fragile skeletons of two babies, who had died at birth or soon after, were also found.

The hill-slope was bisected by a large ditch, its

74 *Early Christian period burial.*

times. Rather than being a prehistoric defence, the bank seems more likely to have resulted from medieval landscaping intended to increase the amount of level ground available for building or cultivation on the hilltop.

As might be expected from a monastic site occupied over many centuries, finds from the three seasons of excavation were prolific. Thirteenth-century wares from the local kiln were recognized, but petrological examination of pottery fabrics indicated that other kilns must have been fired in the area. Imported pottery was rare, although a sherd of 'E ware' from the Continent, conventionally dated to the 7th century AD, was an interesting early example. Butchered animal bones will provide valuable information about animal breeding, butchery techniques and diet. Some bones had been worked into combs, thin slivers of bone riveted together and incised with simple decoration; others had been shaped into toggles and spindle-whorls. One bizarre discovery was part of a vertebra of a whale, a massive disc of bone which found a final use as a slab in an Early Christian period pavement. Perhaps the unfortunate creature stranded itself on the nearby Co Down shore, something which was recorded in the annals as a miraculous event.

Items of simple jewellery were commonly found on the site. Long bronze pins, moulded or incised with a variety of decorations, bronze finger rings, some inset with glass 'stones', bracelets carved from lignite, plain and polychrome glass beads, all show that people were happy to adorn themselves. As well as for building, stone was

75 *Stone with practice interlace ornament.*

profile V-shaped, over 3 m wide and 2 m deep. Dated to the Early Christian period by pottery fragments in the soils which had gradually filled it, the ditch was re-cut on a smaller scale in the medieval period. The ditch probably doubled as a defensive barrier and the formal enclosure for the monastic settlements of both periods on Cathedral Hill. Similar ditches have been recognized on other ecclesiastical sites: air photography has revealed one at the nearby early church on Inch Island, across the river Quoile.

The discovery of the ditch brought into question the long-held identification of the hilltop earthwork as the remains of a Bronze Age hill-fort. Running across the contour, rather than with it, projection of the line of the ditch took it *underneath* the visible earthwork. Accordingly, the bank must have been constructed at a later date, and excavations across its line confirmed that it largely consisted of soils which had built up in medieval often shaped to make whetstones, while two simple flat slabs were found, one used as a practice piece for the carving of interlace ornament (*Fig 75*), the other scratched with lines to make a board game. The oldest object recovered from the site was also of stone, a Neolithic polished axe made from Co Antrim porcellanite. It is tempting to imagine that this prehistoric tool, discovered in the 18th-century demolition debris of the medieval building and thousands of years older than its archaeological context, may have been a curiosity belonging to a medieval cleric.

NFB

28. UNCOVERING THE PAST IN A BUSY TOWN

CARRICKFERGUS
Co Antrim

J 413875

Although Carrickfergus is sometimes claimed to have been founded in the Early Christian period, rescue excavations throughout the 1970s by Tom Delaney* failed to locate any evidence for a settlement of that date. The medieval town developed around the Anglo-Norman castle and St Nicholas' church, the only two buildings to have survived from the medieval period. Excavation has, however, revealed many aspects of life in the town from the late 12th century onwards.

For the earlier medieval period, the late 12th and 13th centuries, perhaps the most significant discovery was a potter's kiln at Irish Quarter (*Fig 76*). The kiln still contained some of the com-

76   Potter's kiln at Irish Quarter.

---

* Tom Delaney died in 1979. The excavations were completed by Lesley Simpson who is preparing a report on the 1970s excavations.

plete vessels abandoned within it after a terminal fault in the firing process. One of only two medieval kilns yet known in Ireland, the range of vessel shapes and local clays used in the pots provide a valuable guide to identifying Carrickfergus wares amongst the thousands of sherds of pottery found in the excavations. Iron- and bone-working also took place in the town, industries revealed largely by the waste products of slag and shaped fragments of bone.

Unlike some Ulster towns, the excavations yielded numbers of medieval coins: of John de Courcy (invader of Ulster in 1177 and the first builder of the castle), Richard I, John and Henry III. These testify to early commercial activity, and the role of Carrickfergus as a European trading port is highlighted by some of the more unusual discoveries – a pottery trumpet from southern France, a pottery cicada (insect) perhaps from the Mediterranean, and the skeleton of a Barbary ape from North Africa or Gibraltar (*Fig 77*). Two sherds of Roman pottery, one of them dated to the 2nd century AD, were found in medieval layers. They may have been relics or keepsakes brought to Ireland by returning pilgrims, or perhaps they were inadvertently dug up in a British or European port in soil used for a ship's ballast, only to be dumped on arrival in Carrickfergus.

The remains of some of Carrickfergus' medieval townsfolk have been found in two locations, both ecclesiastical. In Market Place the discovery of burials suggested that St Nicholas' graveyard was once larger than it is today, while in Joymount, on

77 Skeleton of Barbary ape.

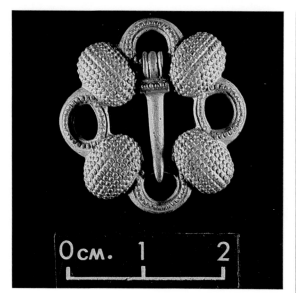

78 Early 13th-century gilded brooch.

the other side of the medieval town, numerous graves were found next to the walls of the Franciscan friary, founded in the 13th century. Some of the jewellery and other possessions lost by such people have been found elsewhere in the town (*Fig 78*).

While no early medieval houses have been found, the defences enclosing the town have been located. At Joymount a large ditch which probably defended the medieval settlement was replaced in the late 16th century by a 'vamour of turf and sods', a rampart and ditch completed in 1574. In this late medieval period wealthier townsfolk looked to their own defences, and contemporary picture-maps show stone tower-houses throughout the town. The foundations of two such buildings were excavated in Cheston Street and High Street, and property leases suggest that they were owned by Robert Sendall and William Dobbin respectively.

The impact made on Carrickfergus by Sir Arthur Chichester, politician and planter, can still be seen in the early 17th-century town wall, particularly well preserved in the north-eastern corner of the town. The Irish Gate and part of the wall on the west side of the town were demolished in the 18th century. Their foundations were uncovered by excavation and have now been preserved and displayed, while the facing of the north bastion was also recovered and restored. A 17th-century ditch found outside the wall at Irish Gate has not been encountered elsewhere, and it seems likely that it was used primarily for drainage rather than defence. Two frames of timber beams at Joymount, remarkably preserved when excavated, are thought to have been platforms for the mounting of guns, used to defend the town while the building of the town wall was being completed.

There has been no excavation of Chichester's grand house, Joymount, remains of which may yet lie beneath the council yard, behind the town hall, although excavations in the grounds to the rear of Joymount unearthed numerous artifacts probably discarded by the household.

Throughout Carrickfergus finds of 17th-century date reveal the contacts that the port continued to enjoy. Imports of pottery from north Devon, one source of settlers in the Ulster Plantation (including Chichester himself), also reveal a transatlantic trade. A 1680–1 port book of Barnstaple, Devon, records that the 'Seraphim' of

Barnstaple called at Carrickfergus on the way to Virginia, the source of tobacco, and thousands of clay tobacco pipes of this period have been found in the town. Coins were in short supply in 17th-century Ireland and many foreign coins circulated, including Scottish, French and Spanish coins and weights. Local merchants issued tokens, amongst them Andrew Willoughby, mayor of Carrickfergus in 1683.

The range of excavated iron objects is large, from nails and horseshoes to knives, Jew's harps and cannon-balls. Numerous leather shoes and off-cuts came from a ditch near Irish Gate, refuse perhaps from a workshop of one of three cobblers named in 17th-century town records. Bird bottles, the ceramic equivalent of wooden nesting boxes, and perhaps made in Spain, were found at Joymount.

The large-scale rescue work of the 1970s has ceased, although a watching brief is still kept on redevelopment proposals for the town. Over the last few years work has concentrated on processing and interpreting the huge archive of records and finds generated by the excavations, and it is hoped that a publication of the results will appear before long.

MLS
NFB

Simpson, M L et al, 'An early 13th-century double-flued pottery kiln at Carrickfergus, County Antrim', Medieval Ceramics 3 (1979), 41–52.
Simpson, M L and Dickson, A, 'Excavations in Carrickfergus, County Antrim', Medieval Archaeology 25 (1981), 78–89.

29. GRIM FORTRESS OR PICTURESQUE RUIN?

GREENCASTLE
Co Down

J 246119
State care

The ruins of this mid 13th-century castle are strategically and picturesquely sited at the seaward end of Carlingford Lough against the background of the Mourne Mountains. It was built at royal expense, probably in an effort to secure a route into Ulster from Leinster and the centre of Anglo-Norman authority in Dublin by ferry from Carlingford. In Ulster the Normans occupied only the east of counties Antrim and Down and in times of war the land route from the south through the Gap of the North was easily disrupted by the Irish.

The remains (Fig 79), comprise a quadrilateral ward surrounded by a curtain wall, with a D-plan angle tower (of differing design) at each corner. A large rectangular residential keep, now the most striking feature of the castle, stands in the northern half of the ward. This building was altered at various times in the Middle Ages and the castle was occupied by the English administration and the Earls of Ulster down to the 17th century, but it had a stormy history and was taken and wrecked by the Irish of Mourne on several recorded occasions. The outer defences, made up of the curtain wall, rock-cut ditch and bank, appear to have fallen into decay at an early stage and were never fully refurbished.

When the castle came into State care (once again) in the 1960s the site was covered by a farmyard which still occupies a strip on the west. The buildings were in urgent need of conservation, the site was full of recent debris and the layout of the angle towers and entrance was obscure. The entrance probably lay on the south, beside the south-west angle tower, where there are stone foundations outside the line of the ditch. In order to clarify the plan of the castle and to help in its presentation to the public a series of research excavations was carried out from time to time in the 1960s and 70s. These revealed a large body of detailed information about the construction and layout of the buildings and, from the depth of stratification and small finds, evidence for events

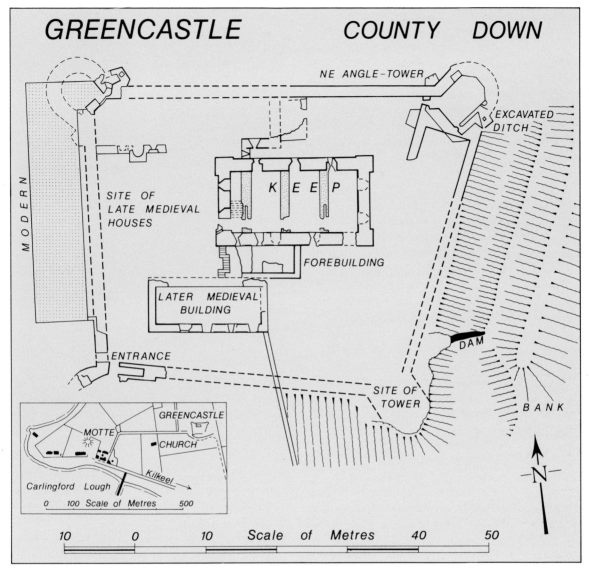

GREENCASTLE   COUNTY DOWN

NE ANGLE-TOWER

EXCAVATED DITCH

MODERN

SITE OF
LATE MEDIEVAL
HOUSES

K E E P

FOREBUILDING

LATER MEDIEVAL
BUILDING

ENTRANCE

DAM

SITE OF
TOWER

B A N K

GREENCASTLE

MOTTE

CHURCH

Kilkeel

Carlingford Lough

0   100 Scale of Metres   500

10   0   10   Scale of Metres   40   50

N

79   Plan of Greencastle with location map (inset).

which took place in and around the castle. Only a few of the more interesting aspects of the 1970s excavations can be dealt with here.

The north-east and south-east angle towers were fully excavated. The masonry of the ground floor of the north-east tower was complete, but the plan of that on the south-east had to be reconstructed from fragments. The outline of a forebuilding, protecting a first floor entrance to the keep, was recovered from excavated foundations immediately to the south. The presence of a massive rock-cut ditch, running immediately outside the line of the curtain wall, was confirmed under

the fields on the north and east and under the farmyard on the south.

The largest operation was the complete excavation of the rock-cut ditch on the east side. This was carried out to present part of the ditch, everywhere filled up level with the surrounding land, to public view. Altogether the excavated part of the ditch was 40 m long, 7.5 m wide and 3.5 m deep. Together with a substantial outer bank the ditch contained stratified deposits spanning the period from the building of the castle to the early 17th century. Hundreds of artifacts were found, mostly pottery and iron implements, and dating mainly from the 14th and 15th centuries. The most interesting evidence, however, relates (in conjunction with written sources) to the construction and early history of the castle.

Documentary references can play a major part in dating activity at medieval sites. Before excavation it was thought that Greencastle was nearing completion in 1260, in which year the exchequer account for Ulster (one of few surviving for this period) mentions the roofing of the keep (*aula turris*) at Greencastle and the manufacture of covered wooden wall-walks (*hurdicia*). The excavation of the ditch demonstrated that the curtain wall had been destroyed deliberately shortly after the castle was completed. We know this because the remains of the original battlements lay directly on a layer of gravel in the ditch bottom, on which also rested a 3 m-high masonry dam spanning the ditch at a point where the rock fell away sharply around the south-east corner. The dam, which was planned from the outset, suggests that the builders hoped (vainly) to retain water around most of the perimeter. The dam was covered in so quickly, however, by the mass of tumbled masonry from the top of the curtain wall that the original masons' trowel-marks were visible on the mortar on its face. Similarly, the original plaster on the undersides of the jumbled blocks of masonry in the ditch was perfectly preserved, but the upper sides of the same blocks were very weathered. This shows that the rubble lay exposed in the ditch bottom for a long time before it was covered by the first of many dumps of rubbish, probably in the 14th or 15th century (*Fig 80*). One of the dumps of fill at the north end of the ditch contained artifacts and debris probably representing the dumped remains of a burnt building which had stood against the inside of the curtain wall. Masses of masonry were also found in trial excavations across the ditch on the south and north sides and it became clear – surprisingly – that the castle had been made indefensible not long after it was constructed.

Surely an event so important as the slighting of a new royal castle would have been recorded, and a search of the medieval annals quickly revealed the following entry: 1260 *Arx viridis in Ultonia prosternitur* (The green fortress in Ulster thrown to the ground). Re-reading of the exchequer account for 1260 showed that Greencastle (along with other Ulster castles) was *repaired* in that year. Whether the repair was carried out before (in anti-

80 Rock-cut ditch partly excavated, showing rubble and midden layers.

cipation of the Irish attack on east Down in 1260 led by Brian O'Neill and Hugh O'Connor) or after the demolition is not clear. While the curtain wall may have been repaired after this event it is certain that the ditch was not cleaned out.

Several documentary references to Greencastle in the 1250s were also discovered, the earliest in 1252 when the justiciar (chief officer of state in Ireland) was ordered to pay Adam Talebot what he had expended in custody of 'Greencastle of the King'. While the chain of circumstances which led to this adjustment of chronology by a decade or so, and the likely discovery of tangible remains of the troubles of the 1260s, is certainly interesting, the most significant conclusion archaeologically is that all of the finds found in the ditch bottom under the rubble (though not numerous, mostly fragments of glazed pottery jugs) can be dated to the 1250s. Similarly, medieval sherds found in a quarry pit and mixed up in the external bank can be dated to

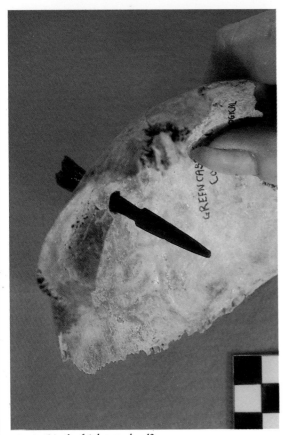

81 Is this the fatal arrowhead?

material for academic studies! One of the objects was a large part of the frontal bone of a human skull with a small neat hole, slightly pointed oval in shape, punched above the brow. The bone was not shattered around the inside of the wound and it was clear that this injury had occurred in antiquity and that it had been caused by a projectile, probably a pointed iron arrowhead. Several other fragments of skulls were found in the ditch at the same level but there were no other human bones. It can be suggested that these represent the remains of the heads of luckless attackers which, exhibited high on the castle wall, when decayed, fell into the ditch. No further thought was given to this find until several years later when some corroded iron scraps, found near the perforated skull fragment in the same layer, were returned after cleaning and conservation. One of the objects turned out to be a carefully-made and decorated, armour-piercing arrowhead with a blunted tip. The first attempt to insert the object into the hole in the skull was unsuccessful and it seemed that this was not the weapon which had caused the fatal injury over 500 years ago. But when the arrowhead was gently rotated in the hole in the skull it suddenly dropped right in, the slight barbs on the arrowhead corresponding exactly with the pointed outline of the entry hole (*Fig 81*). The specimens were submitted to the Belfast Forensic Science Laboratory and the staff reported that they had never seen such good correlation between an injury and a suggested weapon, only regretting that we had not tested the arrowhead for traces of bone before conservation and before trying it through the hole in the skull! The owner of the skull may have been wounded from the very wall on which his head soon formed a grisly exhibit.

CJL

the time of the construction of the castle, probably in about 1250. It is rare to find medieval material in a context which can be safely dated historically to within such narrow limits, and it seems likely that the pottery from these levels at Greencastle will be valuable for working out a chronology of medieval pottery types in Ireland.

Two finds from higher levels in the ditch, perhaps dating to the 14th or 15th century, vividly evoke an incident which may have been unremarkable in the history of the castle but which brings home to us the fact that such places were not designed either as picturesque ruins or raw

Waterman, D M and Collins, A E P, 'Excavations at Greencastle, County Down, 1951', *Ulster J Archaeol* 15 (1952), 87–102.
Gaskell Brown, C, 'Excavations at Greencastle, County Down, 1966–1970', *Ulster J Archaeol* 42 (1979), 51–65.

TILDARG
Co Antrim

J 239965
Scheduled

On the south slope of Big Collin mountain, north-west of Ballyclare, stands a large rectangular earth-work (*Fig 82*). It is extremely well preserved, no doubt largely resulting from its remoteness from modern settlement and its location at an altitude of almost 275 m (900 ft), above the limits of field enclosure. Superficially, the site resembles an earthen bawn, or cattle enclosure, a type of mon-ument most common in the 17th century. In a Plantation context, however, bawns are generally associated with sites of permanent settlement, close to rivers, and the remote location of the

82 Plan of earthwork enclosure.

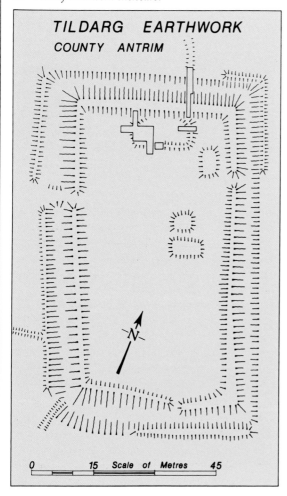

Tildarg earthwork suggested that this was an unlikely explanation.

When interest in the site was aroused during the course of archaeological survey in Co Antrim it emerged that little was known about it except that it was mentioned in passing in late 19th-century surveys. Fortunately, a valuable guide to dating the site was then discovered: it had been referred to as 'the old fort of Tullaghdarge' in two land grants of 1606 and 1609. Clearly, then, the site pre-dated the early 17th century.

In 1982 a small sampling excavation was mounted to try to gain a better understanding of this unusual monument. The excavation was mini-mal because the site was in no danger of destruct-ion, and only four small trenches were opened at the north end of the earthwork. The first trench, cut through the bank and external ditch which formed the enclosure, yielded some details of the earthwork's construction and its subsequent eros-ion but failed to provide any evidence of date or function.

The other trenches, however, sited on a low rectangular mound which overlooked the interior of the enclosure, and which had already been interpreted as the probable site of a building, were more rewarding, generating results which were both unusual and thought-provoking (*Fig 83*). The building was about 16 m long and 6 m wide, rect-angular in plan but with rounded corners. The surviving wall-bases were built of clay and sods, and were unlikely ever to have been very high. There appeared to be no internal partitions, and the single large room was probably heated at the west end by a hearth, exposed as a spread of ashes on the floor. Nearby, a gap in the south wall marked a probable entrance. A radiocarbon date indicated that the ashes of the fire, and so the use of the building, probably dated to the later 13th century.

The hearth, and fragments of coarse, medi-eval pottery on the floor, were enough to identify the remains as a house used for human habitation. A crucial question, however, and one which is not

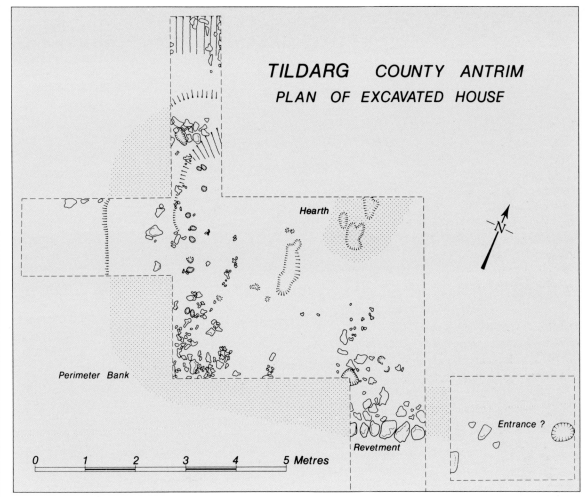

TILDARG   COUNTY ANTRIM
PLAN OF EXCAVATED HOUSE

Hearth

Perimeter Bank

Revetment

Entrance ?

0   1   2   3   4   5 Metres

83   Plan of excavated west end of house.

always answerable by archaeological means, is how was the roof supported? Since drystone-walling was used to revet the earthwork bank, its absence in the house walls would seem to have been intentional, and it can be suggested that the house's low earthen walls were not intended to bear the weight of a roof. The excavations, however, found no traces of the earthfast walling posts necessary to support a roof, and the final interpretation arrived at was that crucks were used: long, curving timbers which rise from the ground surface to the full height of the roof.

While the existence of cruck building in medieval times has been deduced from late medieval Irish pictorial maps and from references in written sources, the Tildarg house, dated by its hearth ashes to the earlier medieval period, is the first

excavated house suggested as having been roofed with crucks. Not surprisingly, such an interpretation will need to be tested by other excavations and confirmed elsewhere before it can enter the mainstream of Irish medieval archaeology.

The interpretation of the earthwork as an animal enclosure, based largely on its appearance, is also supported by the evidence for the medieval Irish practice of transhumance, the periodic migration of cattle and their keepers to upland pastures (*see also p 37*). The problem remains, however, that sites like the Tildarg enclosure are rare in the Irish landscape, while transhumance, at least according to the documentary sources for the later medieval period, was common in an economy where pastoralism was important. The suggested use of (potentially portable) crucks in what

71

appears to have been a little-used building, arguing from the scant pottery remains, could support the idea of occasional use.

Another question arising from the excavation concerns the weather. The site is very high and may well have been ideal upland summer pasture in the 13th century, but was its abandonment the result of deteriorating climate? Research in Britain has traced a pattern of long-term climatic fluctuations, and their probable effect on settlement.

The 12th and 13th centuries were periods of favourable weather, whilst the 14th century saw a marked decline. It is possible that the Tildarg earthwork, situated on what is now marginal upland, was a victim of the same 14th-century climatic deterioration.

NFB

Brannon, N F, 'A small excavation in Tildarg townland, near Ballyclare, County Antrim', *Ulster J Archaeol* 47 (1984), 163–170.

31. TWO MEDIEVAL ABBEYS REDISCOVERED

MUCKAMORE ABBEY AND MASSEREENE FRIARY   J 167855 and J 146866
Co Antrim

Massereene and Muckamore are familiar today as the names of two important south Antrim hospitals. In the medieval period, however, both places were famous for institutions concerned with spiritual care. Indeed, Muckamore Abbey Hospital stands near the priory site, but how many local residents have wondered what and where the original 'abbey' was? By a strange coincidence the ruins of the ecclesiastical buildings at both Massereene and Muckamore, unseen for centuries, were rediscovered in rescue excavations in 1973.

Muckamore Abbey   State care

An Early Christian monastery was founded at Muckamore in about 600 by St Colmán Elo, but there are no contemporary documentary references to the site until 1183, when a prior of Muckamore witnessed a charter of John de Courcy. At about this time the abbey was endowed (or refounded) by the Norman followers of de Courcy who occupied lands in the Sixmilewater valley. In a 14th-century source the names of some of the benefactors are given as William Mataland, Stephen de Sandal, Gilbert de Croft and John Bisset. The priory became wealthy, possessing lands and churches from Dunadry to Islandmagee and north to Ballymena. It was dedicated to SS Mary and Colmán Elo, and its clergy had pastoral

duties following the Augustinian rule as amended at the abbey of St Victor in Paris.

Although no identifiable part of the abbey survived above ground its approximate site was well known. Nineteenth-century sources record the supposed discovery in the area of weapons, coins, silver candlesticks and two 'golden tables', as well as the presence underground of foundations on an improbably large scale. The abbey site was enclosed in a bend of the Sixmilewater, one mile east of Antrim town, in what became a walled garden of Muckamore Abbey Hospital, where the road from Belfast along the 'seven-mile-straight' now meets the important link to the airport. The site was marked with the usual cross on the Ordnance Survey maps and a couple of large pieces of masonry in the garden wall, 3 m high and of doubtful antiquity, were pointed out as the last surviving remnants of the medieval buildings. The trial excavations took place in advance of a road-widening scheme across the site, planned to help heavy lorries at the difficult junction.

The investigator of a ruined or destroyed medieval abbey is aided by the fact that most conformed to a 'conventual layout'. The buildings were arranged with the church aligned east–west at the north (or sometimes the south) side of an open rectangular space, the cloister, surrounded by a covered arcaded walk against the church and against the three domestic ranges. On the east

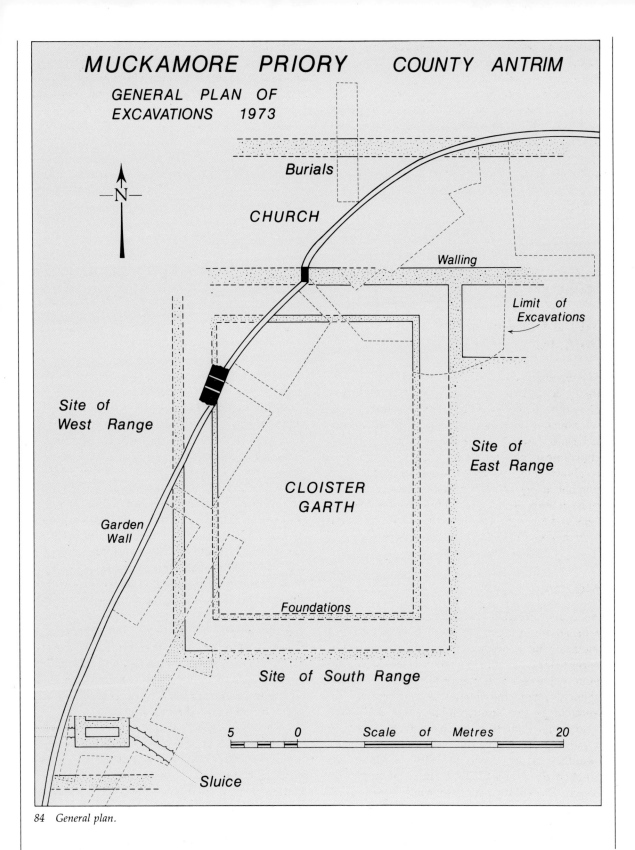

MUCKAMORE PRIORY   COUNTY ANTRIM

GENERAL PLAN OF
EXCAVATIONS 1973

Burials

—N—

CHURCH

Walling

Limit of
Excavations

Site of
West Range

Site of
East Range

CLOISTER
GARTH

Garden
Wall

Foundations

Site of South Range

5   0   Scale   of   Metres   20

Sluice

84   General plan.

73

were the sacristy, chapter room and first floor dormitory; on the south were refectory and kitchen and on the west, workshops and stores. Every part of the abbey could be reached from the cloister and the inward-looking arrangement minimized the need for contact with the outside world. The layout and scale varied, depending among other things on the order involved, the wealth of the foundation and the access to running water. A characteristic feature was the provision of a covered stream to provide fresh water where it entered the abbey and to sluice away waste from the kitchen and latrine blocks, which were usually located at the south ends of the domestic ranges.

The advantage of the conventual layout for the excavator, provided identifiable foundations survive, is that a few strategically-placed trenches can quickly reveal the general plan of the building, and the positions of unexcavated (or destroyed) walls can be estimated fairly accurately. This is exactly what happened at Muckamore, although the excavation was almost stopped after two weeks for lack of results!

The first trench was laid out to examine the foundations of a thick mass of masonry, pierced by an arched opening, incorporated in the garden wall close to the spot indicated on the Ordnance Survey map as the site of the abbey. This revealed a depth of 1.5 m of relatively modern build-up, which presumably was dumped to make up the garden. At the bottom of the trench was a thin soil layer, containing a few sherds of medieval pottery, and this rested on subsoil. The large block of masonry rested on the build-up and it was clearly a recent feature, perhaps built to mark the reputed site of the abbey but certainly not part of it.

The excavated area was extended slightly and a thin wall with a sloping east face was found running north–south under the modern walling. The early wall was about 80 cm high and rested on subsoil. A gully, probably formed by drips from the roof of the cloister walk, containing several rusty nails ran parallel to its east face. A little further excavation confirmed that this was the supporting wall for the cloister arcade on the west. The first trial-trench, on the poor results of which the excavation was almost abandoned, had been opened in the featureless cloister garth! It was clear that extensive ruins of the abbey of Muckamore had been covered up and preserved in laying out the garden, perhaps in the early 19th century.

Further test-trenches revealed enough to reconstruct an outline plan of many of the buildings following the standard conventual layout (*Fig 84*). The aisleless church on the north side was more than 25 m long, and in places its walls were marked only by the absence of burials which had been made while the structure was standing. It was clear that the kink in the garden wall was caused by the fact that the south wall of the church was still standing when the garden wall was built, and a thin column of the church wall survived to a height of 3 m in the garden wall (*Fig 85*). The cloister garth measured 14 m east–west by 21 m north–south and the surrounding walkway was 2.2 m wide. Part of the interior of the north end of the east range of buildings was uncovered. A small stream in a crude boulder-lined channel, which presumably also drained the kitchen area, was

85 Thin column of church wall surviving in garden wall with excavated foundation below.

86 *Pennies of Edward I and II with farthing of de Courcy at centre.*

directed under the south end of the west range in an arched culvert. The silt in the drain contained numerous sherds of fine medieval pottery, bronze and iron objects and nineteen coins, fifteen of which from the upper silt layers could represent part of a dispersed group of coins of early 14th-century date (*Fig 86*). Fragments of window lead, the feet of cast bronze cooking pots, an iron spear-head, fragments of painted plaster and animal bones were also found in the sluice.

A farthing of John de Courcy (*Fig 86, centre*) was found in a shallow feature running under the west cloister arcade wall indicating that this part of the abbey had been constructed after the loss of the coin, which probably occurred in the 1190s. No trace of Early Christian activity was found, but the medieval priory could well have been laid out to one side of an earlier site.

This small excavation was dramatically successful in discovering and elucidating the remains of Muckamore abbey. The Department of the Environment Roads Service amended its plans to avoid disturbing those parts of the ruins which lie under the enlarged road (the west range of domestic buildings and the west end of the church) and to minimize the encroachment of a new footpath over the site. The owners of the garden, the Northern Ireland Hospitals Authority, kindly sold the area of the garden occupied by the ruins to HMBB for a nominal sum. The exposed walls and foundations have been covered in, but all of the site not occupied by the road is now in State care and awaits future excavation and display.

Massereene Friary

Beneath the embankment of a new by-pass on the west side of Antrim town lie the excavated remains of a small friary of the Franciscan Third Order Regular, reputedly founded in about 1500 by Phelim O'Neill. The 'site of abbey' was marked on the Ordnance Survey map in a strip of woodland on the south bank of the Sixmilewater river, exactly in the line of the proposed road. It was impossible to have the road line moved and it was decided to do a trial excavation on this site in 1973 because little was known of the archaeology of Ulster's once numerous Third Order friaries. Other late medieval Third Order friaries in Co Antrim, also founded under the patronage of ruling Gaelic families, existed at Lambeg, Larne and Glenarm, but significant remains survive only at Bonamargy (in State care) near Ballycastle. It was considered important to see if the foundations of buildings and contemporary archaeological deposits could be traced at Massereene.

Several days were spent in opening featureless trial trenches among the trees where the reputed sites was marked on the map. The excavation was about to be abandoned when a local resident, whose garden backed onto the site, showed us where he recollected finding mortar and stones in his onion patch! A few minutes digging here revealed the line of an old masonry wall and the area of excavation was at once shifted to a spot in open ground immediately outside the garden on the west. Here the foundations and some lower walling of a small, simple church were soon exposed (*Fig 87*). In 1974 it was possible to strip rapidly the complete outline of the church and part of the domestic range on the east because the adjacent house and garden had by then been vacated to make way for the road. The church was a plain rectangle, 30 m long and 8.5 m wide externally (*Fig 88*). The walls had been robbed out for most of their length to the level of a broad irregular foundation. The interior was full of disturbed shallow burials and garden loam and there was no sign of an original floor. Several of the burials at the west end appeared to have been

87 *West end of church from south.*

deposited unceremoniously at one time, and all probably are later than the period when the building was used as a friary church.

A stone-built drain ran parallel to the outside of the church gable on the east, evidently leading towards the river, 50 m to the north. Foundations of a domestic range running southwards were attached to those of the church at the east end. It seems certain that a full conventual layout did not exist at Massereene and that the buildings were laid out to an L-shaped plan with the church on the north and a domestic range on the east.

Outside the west end of the church an unexpected series of ditches and trenches was found. The earliest was a wide, irregular, V-sectioned ditch, 3 m wide and 2 m deep, which ran north–

88 *General plan.*

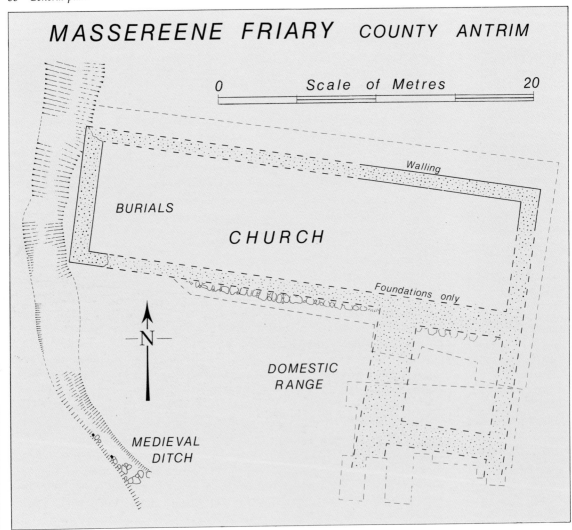

MASSEREENE FRIARY COUNTY ANTRIM

0   Scale of Metres   20

BURIALS

CHURCH

Walling

Foundations only

—N—

DOMESTIC RANGE

MEDIEVAL DITCH

south very close to the west end of the church. When the ditch had half silted up it was roughly paved over at one point to re-establish access to the church, which may have been derelict by this time. A number of interesting finds came from the lowest fill of the ditch. These included an iron plough sock with the coulter pushed into it (*Fig 89*), sherds of local, hand-made cooking pottery, some green-glazed sherds thought to be of 16th-century Scottish type and a stack of eleven silver coins corroded together. Among the Irish and English groats and half groats was a *double patard* of Charles the Bold of Burgundy (1467–77). The coins indicated that the ditch had been dug and the friary constructed shortly before about 1505. Some of the later ditches may have been dug after the friary was abandoned in the later 16th century. A scattered group of eleven pennies of 1601 at the base of topsoil inside the church suggests, however, that the site remained in use at this time. Archaeological and documentary evidence combine to indicate that the friary ruins may have been used as a temporary fort or staging-post in the Elizabethan campaign against the Ulster clans north and west of Lough Neagh, but the historic 'fort of Massereene' is thought to have stood nearer the mouth of the Sixmilewater.

The excavations brought to light the outline of a late medieval friary and amplified its history before it disappeared for ever. The information we now have about the scale and layout of this friary can be added to the small amount already available for these religious institutions, which can be recognized and valued as an important element of civilization and patronage in later medieval Ulster, often overlooked by modern commentators. Another valuable conclusion is that much of the excavated material can be dated securely to the 16th century. So here, at Massereene, the decision to mount a salvage excavation on a featureless site, recorded only on the Ordnance Survey maps, was amply rewarded.

CJL

McKeown, L, 'The abbey of Muckamore', *J Down and Connor Historical Society* 9 (1938), 63–70.

89   Early 16th-century plough sock and coulter (length 48 cm).

COLERAINE
Co Londonderry

C 284432

Excavations in Coleraine began in 1978, when major public housing and car-parking developments threatened a townscape which had originated in the 1610–11 'plantation' by the London Companies. In the years up to 1984 a dozen sites were excavated, revealing the remains of 17th-century houses, the town's earthwork defences and central fortress, and yielding rubbish pits containing household goods discarded by Coleraine townsfolk centuries ago.

Written and pictorial records of Coleraine in the 17th and 18th centuries are of such quality (*Fig 90*) that many of the archaeologists' discoveries can be linked with them to build up a comprehensive picture of historic Coleraine, a process known as historical archaeology.

'A good rampier [rampart] of earth and sods' defended the town boundary in 1611, but eleven years later one critic complained that the 'earthen fortification dailie decayeth'. By 1738 these urban defences had all but vanished, but their line, as today, had been enshrined in property boundaries. Excavations south of Ferryquay Street confirmed that the 'rampier' had indeed decayed, the layers of soil and gravel used in its construction having dramatically eroded over the 1611 ground surface beneath (*Fig 91*).

To the north, on the other side of the street, a

91   The 1611 rampart.

massive stone wall, almost 2 m thick, was discovered, and traced for over 30 m towards the riverside. This was Coleraine's 'citadel', or inner fortification, built around 1630 and demolished by 1670. Soils rich with rubbish – potsherds and animal bones – had built up against the wall and were sealed with a thick layer of demolition debris, which conveniently provided a limit of pre-1670 for the dating of the finds. While the 'citadel' was too large for extensive excavation to be practicable, the lines of its walls were traced during subsequent development, showing it to have had an unusual triangular ground plan.

The early 17th-century houses of Coleraine were mostly timber-framed (of 'cage-work'), erected as terraces in prefabricated sections, an architectural combination otherwise unknown in Ulster. Over the years there have been occasional 'sightings' of timbers in street frontage developments, but none of these early houses is known to survive above ground. Recent demolition of a modern shop in Church Street revealed the 'silhouette' of one house, most of its timbers having long since vanished but leaving their positions imprinted in the mortar rendering of the shop next door.

In 1981 the discovery that two derelict shops in New Row were once a grand town house, built in 1674, generated great excitement. Much of the

90   Thomas Raven's 1622 map of Coleraine (PRONI).

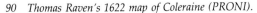
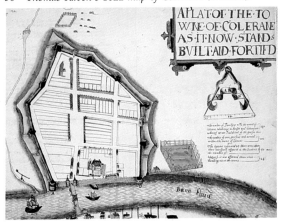

house's fabric, originally of stone, had been replaced by brickwork, but its massive oak roof timbers, shaped from trees felled in 1674, were intact. Dismantling of the house for re-erection in the Ulster Folk Museum laid bare beneath it a ground surface mostly undisturbed for 310 years, a rare occurrence in urban archaeology.

A 1611 survey stated that the site had been occupied by timber-framed houses, 'each tenement 18 foote long and 12 foote wyde . . . some of them with brick chimneys'. Excavation rapidly revealed large stone sills, upon which the timber walls of these houses had been erected on frontage lines surviving to this day. In the middle of one wall lay the remains of a brick fireplace, blackened from use. The excavated dimensions matched those recorded in 1611.

At the rear of the 1674 house the excavators uncovered a large stone-lined rubbish pit full of broken crockery, wine bottles and glasses, clay tobacco pipes and wig-curlers, along with animal bones and sea-shells discarded after meals. Many of the pottery vessels were English imports, from Staffordshire (*Fig 92*), London and Devon, dating from the early 1700s. Records show the house to have been leased around 1733 to Thomas Mayors,

92 *Early 18th-century Staffordshire slipwares.*

an apothecary, and it is tempting to imagine that much of this rubbish was dumped in the pit when Mayors moved in.

NFB

Robinson, P S and Brannon, N F, 'A seventeenth-century house in New Row, Coleraine', *Ulster J Archaeol* 44 & 45 (1981–2), 173–178.
Robinson, P S, 'Some late survivals of box-framed "Plantation" houses in Coleraine, County Londonderry', *Ulster J Archaeol* 46 (1983), 129–136.

33. IN SEARCH OF OLD BELFAST

BELFAST
J 338743 and J 340744

In November 1983 the demolition of a city-centre store provided archaeologists with a brief opportunity to examine the buried evidence of historic Belfast, and for the first time the chance was seized (*Fig 93*). It also gave the people of Belfast a chance to watch the archaeologists at work. Seven days were made available to excavate the site in search of Sir Arthur Chichester's 17th-century fortified house. Lord Deputy Chichester, one of the chief architects of the Plantation of Ulster, had founded his house on the ruins of an earlier, medieval fortification, and it was destroyed by fire in 1708.

Unlike some towns in Ireland, Belfast's past is poorly represented on historic maps. The most

reliable one, showing the town as it looked in about 1685, depicts Chichester's house standing within enclosed gardens in the area south of present day Castle Place (*Fig 94*). Another map, dated 1660 but of dubious accuracy, depicts an enormous ground plan of the house and in terms of the modern street pattern locates it partly on the available development site at the junction of Castle Lane and Callender Street.

As this was the first controlled archaeological excavation within the city centre it was considered that almost any knowledge or experience gained from the work, for example about the depth and survival of archaeological deposits, the range of

93 Castle Lane: work in progress.

94 Thomas Phillips' 1685 map of Belfast (PRONI).

artifacts or the degree of underground waterlogging, would be valuable in assessing Belfast's archaeological potential.

The streets bordering the excavation site, fossilized today in Castle Arcade and Cornmarket, were first laid out in the 18th century along property alignments which differed from those of Chichester's house and gardens. A long, L-plan trench was therefore laid out parallel to the later streets in anticipation that any remains of 17th-century buildings would stand out in the buried soils. This, indeed, proved to be the case, as brick drains and the foundation trench of a wall were found running diagonally across the trench.

The discovery of Chichester's house, Belfast Castle, however, could not be claimed, and it is probable that the excavation trench, sunk mostly through a thick built-up layer of black soil containing artifacts ranging in date throughout the 17th century, had encountered open ground, perhaps gardens, behind the house. This appears to confirm the probability that Belfast Castle stood on the

north side of Castle Lane, and the '1660' map of Belfast is revealed as an unreliable guide in selecting sites for excavation.

In the summer of 1984 the archaeologists turned their attention to a large car-park in High Street. With more time available for excavation than in 1983, but with a redevelopment site so large that only a sampling project could be contemplated, the first trench, cut along the High Street frontage, rapidly drew a blank. Any evidence for the 17th-century houses that once stood there had been destroyed by the massive brick foundations of later buildings.

Back from the High Street frontage, along the edge of the 18th-century lane known as Pottinger's Entry, a second trench was opened over what had once been 17th-century rear gardens behind the High Street properties. It was hoped that these gardens might contain deep, well-stratified rubbish pits, the 17th-century equivalent of today's dustbins, and often very revealing in their contents.

Under the stone and brick foundations of what had been amongst the first buildings in Pottinger's Entry the excavators' hopes were realized when a large pit was found, the black soil which filled it standing out strongly against the pale green subsoil sand into which it had been cut in the late 17th century. Along with the fragments of British and Continental pottery vessels, bottles, hand-painted window glass and corroded metalwork, the pit contained quantities of animal bones. Superficially unattractive by comparison with the glazed pottery fragments or the iridescent glass, the bones nevertheless provided valuable

95 *Pottinger's Entry: 18th-century family pet?*

dog had decomposed while the pit lay open. A cat's skull, rat bones and a sheep bone still bearing the tooth marks of some gnawing creature, probably a rat, enliven the impression of an insalubrious environment.

Other bones reveal the presence of both native, medieval shorthorn, and introduced, 17th-century longhorn cattle. They also show the wide range of meat eaten, from sirloin and T-bone steaks to skull and toe bones fit only for soup and stock-making. Rabbit bones, a surprising discovery in an urban context, may be the food by-product of a trade in rabbit skins.

In a town where there have been numerous excavations these results could be fitted into a wide interpretation of 17th-century life-style. In the Belfast context, however, where this was only the second excavation ever carried out in the city, interpretations must remain provisional until supplemented by future work. Do the bones represent a good sample? Does the range of high and poor quality cuts of meat indicate a social division in diet (for example between the owners of a house and their servants) or did 17th-century families simply consume a wide range of food? Excavation of further redevelopment sites may fill out the emerging picture.

NFB

information about 17th-century life in Belfast.

The skull of a dog, perhaps once a family pet slightly smaller than a modern setter, lay in the pit, its jaw still articulated as in life (*Fig 95*). While the dog's head had clearly still been flesh-covered when it was thrown into the pit, the scattered disposition of its other bones indicated that the

34. A LOST 17th-CENTURY HOUSE RECOVERED

DUNGIVEN
Co Londonderry

C 692083
State care

The demonstration in 1980 that Sir Edward Doddington's 17th-century house and bawn once stood at Dungiven priory and not in Dungiven town provoked a flurry of historical and archaeological reassessment. The wealth of historical information about the site, including contemporary drawings and descriptions, and measured surveys of Doddington's buildings, could now be compared with the standing remains of the priory, which are in State care. The buried structures revealed in previous excavations, assumed to belong to the ecclesiastical occupation, could also

be reconsidered.

Doddington's dwelling, occupied from about 1610, was made up of his newly-built 'fair stone house 46 foot long, 21 foot broad, and 2 stories high slated', the renovated medieval priory church and tower, and ancillary buildings, arranged around a cobbled courtyard to form a defensible enclosure or bawn (*Fig 96*). While the Augustinian priory survives today as a substantial ruin, noted particularly for the late 15th-century knight's tomb in the chancel (Cooey-na-Gall's tomb), the 17th-century buildings had long vanished from the ground floor rooms of the house, defined by 1 m-thick wall stumps which still bore traces of internal plastering. The ground floor of the house consisted of two rooms divided by a central, H-plan chimney (*Fig 97*). Seventeenth-century illustrations show that the house was entered by a porched door in the east wall. Passing through the door a visitor would enter a small lobby, with the stone chimney stack straight ahead, and to either side doors into two rooms, both heated by fireplaces.

The floor of the smaller, southern room was of wooden planks, burnt traces of which were found lying on timber joists. This may have been the parlour, while the northern room, somewhat larger, may have been the kitchen. Butting on to the rear of the house was 'a Returne of stone',

96 *Thomas Raven's 1622 view of priory, house and bawn (PRONI).*

98 *Seventeenth-century iron hinge (height 16.5 cm) (drawing D Warner).*

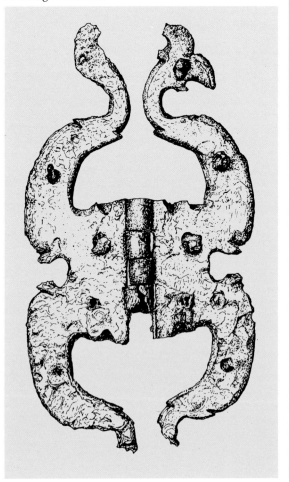

sight and memory of historians and local people. Excavations in the early 1970s had uncovered well-preserved remains of Doddington's house, but these had been reburied, their true identity unrecognized.

In 1982 excavations resumed, with the intention of revealing Doddington's house (including reopening of those parts which were already known), examining its contents, and of gauging the display potential of the 17th-century phase of this well-known State care monument.

The house had been built of stone, and the bulk of the deposits covering its remains consisted of rubble and mortar fragments, clearly derived from the ruin of the building. Though laborious to remove, this thick rubble layer had preserved this part of the site from later damage, unlike the priory grounds nearby which are covered with 18th- and 19th-century graves.

Beneath the rubble lay the remains of the

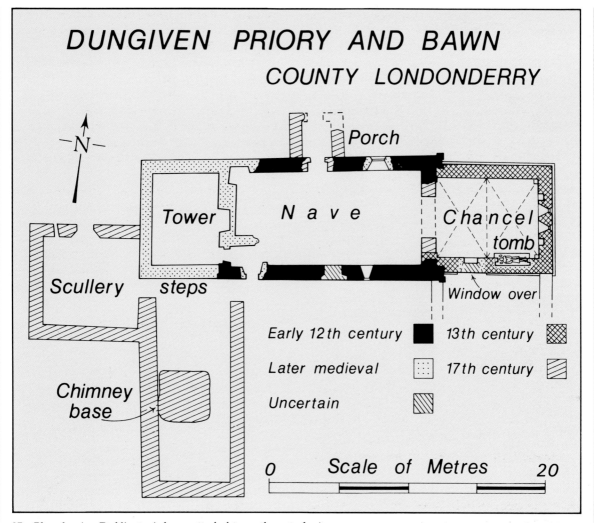

DUNGIVEN PRIORY AND BAWN
COUNTY LONDONDERRY

-N-

Porch

Tower N a v e Chancel

tomb

Scullery steps

Window over

Early 12th century ▇ 13th century ▨

Later medieval ░ 17th century ▨

Uncertain ▨

Chimney base

0 Scale of Metres 20

97 Plan showing Doddington's house attached to south-west of priory.

entered from the house by a flight of sandstone steps and externally by a large doorway from a rear courtyard. Its ground floor was paved with sandstone blocks. A large built-in drain and the absence of a fireplace suggest that this was a scullery.

Traces of a severe fire were found throughout the house. Timber floor joists and planks had been reduced to charcoal, while large, burnt beams, probably roofing timbers, lay on the scullery steps. Other evidence, however, suggests that while a fire probably caused disastrous damage to Doddington's house, it was not an *occupied* house that was burned. The finds from the excavation, such as iron hinges (*Fig 98*), locks, keyhole escutcheons, bolts and nails, represent the furnishings and fittings of the house; they are not the personal possessions of Doddington's household. The walls of the buildings, also, in places located only by the white plaster which marked the line of the inner face, survived in too poor a condition to be interpreted simply as the result of collapse. Rather, the evidence suggests that Doddington's house went out of domestic use and became derelict, that all portable and valuable furnishings were stripped from it, and that parts of the building were deliberately demolished and the stone re-used elsewhere. The house then somehow caught fire, and finally the remains of the building were knocked down or fell.

Sir Edward Doddington died in 1618, but records show that his widow probably continued to live at the site at least until the mid 17th century.

Artifacts recoverd from the ruins appear to be no later than 1660–1670 in date.

No mention of the destruction of the house has been traced in written sources and it may be that perhaps no-one was killed and the occasion was not particularly memorable. Despite its size and local grandeur, the location of Doddington's house and bawn passed out of memory, to be rediscovered over 300 years later. Conservation and presentation of the remains exposed next to the priory will ensure that Doddington's house will not be forgotten again.

NFB

Brannon, N F and Blades, B S, 'Dungiven bawn re-edified', *Ulster J Archaeol* 43 (1980), 91–96.
Brannon, N F, 'Archaeological excavations at Dungiven priory and bawn', *Benbradagh* 15 (1985), 15–18.

Appendix 1

ARCHAEOLOGICAL EXCAVATIONS ORGANIZED BY THE DEPARTMENT OF THE ENVIRONMENT FOR NORTHERN IRELAND 1970–86

The excavations in each year are tabulated alphabetically by county and then townland or the specific place-name of the site. All of the excavations were carried out for rescue purposes in advance of destruction except where (R) appears indicating a 'research' excavation or (C) indicating an excavation carried out in connection with conservation or presentation of a State care monument.

Abbreviations
UJA – *Ulster Journal of Archaeology.*
Meso – Mesolithic.

Neo – Neolithic.
BA – Bronze Age.
IA – Iron Age.
EC – Early Christian.
M – medieval.
PM – post-medieval.
QUB – Queen's University Belfast.
UM – Ulster Museum.
* contracted director.
SC – State care site at time of excavation.
(N) indicates that no archaeological information was retrieved.

Site	Type	Period	Director	Published
1970				
Co Antrim				
Ballyduff	Rath	EC	M Avery (QUB)	
Killealy	Rath	EC	A E T Harper	
Co Armagh				
Armagh City	Friary	M(C)	C J Lynn	*UJA* 1975
Navan	Site B mound (SC)	BA/IA(R)	D M Waterman	
Co Down				
Farrell's Fort, Ballylesson	Rath	EC	A E P Collins	
Greencastle (N and E ditch)	Castle (SC)	M(C)	C J Lynn	
Co Londonderry				
Banagher	Church (SC)	M(C)	C J Lynn/ D M Waterman	*UJA* 1976
Dungiven	Priory and Plantation house (SC)	EC/M/ PM(C)	A E T Harper	
Co Tyrone				
Carnkenny	Ring-cairn	BA	C J Lynn	*UJA* 1973 & 4
Ballynagilly	Settlements	Neo/BA	A M ApSimon (QUB)	

Site	Type	Period	Director	Published
1971				
Co Antrim				
Ballymacrea Lower	Settlement	Neo	A E P Collins	*UJA* 1977
Ballygortgarve	Rath	EC	C J Lynn	*UJA* 1978
Cloughorr	Souterrain	EC	A E T Harper	*UJA* 1972
Poleglass	Rath	EC	A E T Harper	
Seacash	Rath	EC	C J Lynn	*UJA* 1978
Co Armagh				
Lisdrumchor Upper	Rath	?	A E P Collins	
Tullyallan	Rath	?	A E P Collins	
Co Down				
Crossnacreevy	Rath	EC	A E T Harper	*UJA* 1973 & 4
Greencastle (E ditch)	Castle (SC)	M(C)	C J Lynn	
1972				
Co Antrim				
Ballyhenry	Two raths	EC	C J Lynn	*UJA* 1983
Carrickfergus (Market Place, Cheston St, Joymount)	Urban	M/PM	T G Delaney (UM)	
Shane's Castle	Rath	EC	C J Lynn	
Co Down				
Gransha	Rath-mound	EC	C J Lynn	*UJA* 1985 (interim)
Greencastle (S ditch)	Castle (SC)	M(R)	C J Lynn	
1973				
Co Antrim				
Balloo (Massereene)	Friary	M	C J Lynn	
Ballynoe	Rectilinear earthwork	?EC	C J Lynn	*UJA* 1980
Carrickfergus (Joymount and High Street)	Urban	M/PM	T G Delaney (UM)	
Finkiltagh	Rath	EC	B B Williams	
Muckamore	Priory	M	C J Lynn	
Co Down				
Bishopscourt	Souterrain	EC/M	C J Lynn	*UJA* 1979
Grey Abbey	Abbey (SC)	M(C)	A D Bratt	
Co Fermanagh				
Devenish Island	Priory (SC)	M(C)	D M Waterman	*UJA* 1979
Co Londonderry				
Lismurphy	Rath (site of)	?	C J Lynn	*UJA* 1980
Mount Sandel	Settlement	Meso	P C Woodman (UM)	HMSO 1985
Co Tyrone				
Lough Eskragh	Crannogs	BA	B B Williams	*UJA* 1978

Site	Type	Period	Director	Published
1974				
Co Antrim				
Balloo (Massereene)	Friary	M	C J Lynn	
Ballywee	Rath and souterrains	EC	C J Lynn	
Carrickfergus (Joymount and High St)	Urban	M/PM	T G Delaney (UM)	
Dunsilly	Motte and rath	EC/M	T E McNeill (QUB)	
Muckamore	Priory	M	C J Lynn	
Co Fermanagh				
Devenish Island	Priory (SC)	M(C)	D M Waterman	*UJA* 1979
1975				
Co Antrim				
Ballymacaldrack (Dooey's Cairn)	Court tomb	Neo(R)	A E P Collins	*UJA* 1976
Carrickfergus (Joymount and High St)	Urban	M/PM	T G Delaney (UM)	
Deerfin Lower	Enclosure	EC	A D Bratt	
Dunsilly	Motte and rath	EC/M	T E McNeill (QUB)	
Co Armagh				
Armagh (Market St)	Lake fill	M/PM	C J Lynn	
Tray td, 'The King's Stables'	Artificial pond	BA	C J Lynn	*UJA* 1977
Co Fermanagh				
Kiltierney (several sites)	Rath, stone circle, etc	BA/EC	B B Williams M J Daniells	*UJA* 1977
Co Londonderry				
Dungiven	Priory (SC) church	EC/M(C)	A D Bratt	
Dungiven	Standing stone	?	A D Bratt	
Mount Sandel	Mound (SC)	Meso and ?	A E P Collins	*UJA* 1983
1976				
Co Antrim				
Carrickfergus (Joymount, High St, Irish Quarter, Sailor's Row, Castle Green)	Urban	M/PM	T G Delaney (UM)	
Co Armagh				
Armagh (43 Scotch St, 36 Scotch St, Castle St)	Urban	EC/M/PM	C J Lynn	
Co Down				
Ballinran	Court tomb (site of)	Neo	A E P Collins	*UJA* 1976

Site	Type	Period	Director	Published
Co Fermanagh				
Tully	Court tomb	Neo	D M Waterman	*UJA* 1978
Co Londonderry				
Big Glebe	Rath-mound	EC	A D Bratt	
			C J Lynn	

1977

Co Antrim				
Balloo (Massereene)	Friary	M	N F Brannon	
			C J Lynn	
Ballyboley	Souterrain	EC	C J Lynn	
Ballymurphy	Rath	EC	C J Lynn	
Carrickfergus (High St, Irish Quarter)	Urban	M/PM	T G Delaney (UM)	
Co Armagh				
Armagh (36 Scotch St)	Ecclesiastical site	Prehist/ EC/M/PM	C J Lynn	
Dorsey	Linear earthworks/ enclosure	IA	C J Lynn	
Co Down				
Carnalbanagh	Enclosure	EC/M	N F Brannon	*UJA* 1979
Greencastle (forebuilding, etc)	Castle (SC)	M(C)	C J Lynn	
St John's Point	Church (SC)	EC/M(C)	N F Brannon	*UJA* 1980
Co Fermanagh				
Carn	Cashel	EC	N F Brannon	*UJA* 1981 & 2
Kilsmullan	Find spot of axe	BA(R)	B B Williams	*UJA* 1984
Lisdoo	Rath	EC	N F Brannon	*UJA* 1981 & 2
Co Londonderry				
Knockoneill	Court tomb	Neo/BA(R)	L N W Flanagan (UM)	*UJA* 1980 (interim)
Tamnyrankin	Court tomb	Neo(R)	L N W Flanagan (UM)	

1978

Co Antrim				
Carrickfergus (High St, Irish Quarter)	Urban	M/PM	T G Delaney (UM)	
Greencastle	Site of earthworks	PM	N F Brannon	*UJA* 1986
Turraloskin	Pillar-stone	EC	N F Brannon	*UJA* 1979
Co Armagh				
Ballybrolly	Enclosure	EC	C J Lynn	*UJA* 1983
Shewis	Rath	EC	N F Brannon	*UJA* 1980

Site	Type	Period	Director	Published
Co Down				
Lisnagade td (Lisnavaragh)	Rath (SC)	EC(C)(N)	C J Lynn	
Rathmullan	Rath and motte	EC/M	C J Lynn	*UJA* 1981 & 2 *UJA* 1985
Co Londonderry				
Coleraine	Urban	M/PM	N F Brannon	
Mullaboy	Field wall	Prehist	B B Williams	*UJA* 1981 & 2
Co Tyrone				
Beaghmore	Cairn	BA	N F Brannon	*UJA* 1979

1979

Co Antrim

Site	Type	Period	Director	Published
Ballykennedy	Rath	EC	N F Brannon	*UJA* 1980
Carrickfergus (High St, Irish Gate)	Urban	M/PM	M L Simpson*	

Co Armagh

Site	Type	Period	Director	Published
Armagh (37–41, 46 Scotch St)	Ecclesiastical site	Neo/EC/M/PM	C J Lynn	

Co Down

Site	Type	Period	Director	Published
Drumbroneth	Two raths	EC	N F Brannon	*UJA* 1980
Mahee Island (Nendrum)	Monastery (SC)	EC/M(C)	N F Brannon	

Co Fermanagh

Site	Type	Period	Director	Published
Monmurry	Find-spot of armlet	(R)(N)	C J Lynn	

Co Londonderry

Site	Type	Period	Director	Published
Ballygroll	Cairn	Prehist	B B Williams	*UJA* 1981 & 2
Coleraine	Urban	M/PM	N F Brannon	

Co Tyrone

Site	Type	Period	Director	Published
Altanagh	Cairn and rath	Neo/BA/EC	B B Williams	*UJA* 1986
Creggandevesky	Court tomb	Neo	C Foley	
Gallanagh	Tree ring	Recent	B B Williams	*UJA* 1980
Radergan	Megalith	Neo	N F Brannon	*UJA* 1981 & 2

1980

Co Antrim

Site	Type	Period	Director	Published
Ballypalady	Rath	EC	T McErlean*	
Greenisland	Castle Lug	PM	N F Brannon	*UJA* 1981 & 2

Co Armagh

Site	Type	Period	Director	Published
Armagh (37–41 Scotch St)	Urban	Neo/EC/M/PM	C J Lynn J A McDowell*	

Site	Type	Period	Director	Published
Co Down				
Church Quarter (Dundonald)	Motte	M(N)	N F Brannon	
Movilla	Ecclesiastical site	EC/M	M J Yates	*UJA* 1983
Co Londonderry				
Coleraine	Urban	M/PM	N F Brannon	
Macosquin	Ecclesiastical site	M	N F Brannon	*UJA* 1983
Co Tyrone				
Altanagh	Cairn and rath	Neo/BA/EC	B B Williams	*UJA* 1986
Carr	Rath	BA/EC/M	T. McErlean*	
Creggandevesky	Court tomb	Neo	C Foley	
Errigal Keerogue	Church (SC)	M/PM(C)	N F Brannon	
Killycanavan	Rath	EC	T McErlean*	
1981				
Co Antrim				
Carrickfergus (Antrim St)	Urban	M/PM	N F Brannon	
Ballyutoag	Upland settlement	EC(R)	B B Williams	*UJA* 1984
Co Armagh				
Armagh	Cathedral precinct	EC/M(N)	C J Lynn	
Co Down				
Movilla	Ecclesiastical site	EC/M	R J Ivens*	*UJA* 1984
Newtownards	Urban	M/PM	N F Brannon	
Co Fermanagh				
Cloghcor	Stone circle	Prehist	B B Williams M J Yates	*UJA* 1981 & 2
Co Tyrone				
Altanagh	Cairn and rath	Neo/BA/EC	B B Williams	*UJA* 1986
Creggandevesky	Court tomb	Neo	C Foley	
Farrest	Earthwork	?M	C J Lynn	*UJA* 1983
The Bonn	Bawn	PM	N F Brannon	*UJA* 1984
Tremoge	Cist burial	BA	C Foley	*UJA* 1985
1982				
Co Antrim				
Ballyutoag	Hut site, enclosure	Prehist(R)	M J Yates	
Ballyutoag	Upland settlement	EC(R)	B B Williams	*UJA* 1984
Carnaghlis	Rectangular earthwork	?M(R)	B B Williams	
Glenmakeeran	Cist grave, house sites	BA/M	B B Williams	*UJA* 1983

Site	Type	Period	Director	Published
Killylane	Earthworks	EC/PM(R)	B B Williams M J Yates	*UJA* 1984
Tildarg	Rectangular earthwork	M(R)	N F Brannon	*UJA* 1984
Co Down				
Downpatrick (The Grove)	Urban	M	N F Brannon	
Gransha	Rath-mound	EC	C J Lynn	*UJA* 1985 (interim)
Greencastle (SE corner tower)	Castle (SC)	M(C)	C J Lynn	
Inch	Ecclesiastical site	EC/M	N F Brannon	
Co Londonderry				
Dungiven Priory	17th-century house (SC)	PM(C)	N F Brannon	
Co Tyrone				
Creggandevesky	Court tomb	Neo(R)	C Foley	
Derryloran	Church (SC)	M/PM(C)	N F Brannon	*UJA* 1986
Doras	Ecclesiastical enclosure	EC/M	J A McDowell*	
Killyliss	Rath	EC	R J Ivens*	*UJA* 1984
Tamlaght	Rath	(N)	C Foley	

1983

Site	Type	Period	Director	Published
Co Antrim				
Belfast (Castle St)	Urban	M/PM	N F Brannon	
Drumnakeel	Urn burials	BA	B B Williams	*UJA* 1985
Rathlin, Church Bay	Cist graves	BA	K Wiggins*	
Co Armagh				
Armagh (46 Scotch St, garden)	Ecclesiastical site	EC/M/PM	J A McDowell*	
Castleraw	House	PM(R)	N F Brannon	*UJA* 1983
Legarhill	Possible church site	M(N)	C J Lynn	
Co Down				
Ballybeen	Standing stone	BA	J P Mallory (QUB)	*UJA* 1984
Ballyginny	Souterrain	EC	N F Brannon	
Inch	Abbey nave (SC)	M(C)	M Meek	
Maghera	Ecclesiastical enclosure	EC/M	C J Lynn	
Tullylish	Ecclesiastical enclosure	EC/M	R J Ivens*	
Co Fermanagh				
Coolcran	Rath	EC	B B Williams	*UJA* 1985

Site	Type	Period	Director	Published
Killygreagh	Slight earthwork	(N)	C J Lynn	
Kiltierney	Mounds/burials	IA	C Foley	
Co Londonderry				
Brackfield	Bawn (SC)	PM(C)	N F Brannon	
Londonderry City Wall	Water Bastion (SC)	PM	N F Brannon	*UJA* 1986
Dungiven Priory	17th-century house (SC)	PM(C)	N F Brannon	
Knockoneill	Court tomb (SC)	Neo/BA(C)	L N W Flanagan (UM)	
Co Tyrone				
Tullylinton	Site of standing stone	?(N)	M J Yates	*UJA* 1983

1984

Site	Type	Period	Director	Published
Co Antrim				
Ballyhill Lower	Rath	EC	B B Williams	
Ballyvollen	Ironworking site	EC	B B Williams	*UJA* 1985
Ballywee	Rath and souterrains (SC)	EC(C)	C J Lynn	
Carrickfergus (Joymount)	Town wall (SC)	M/PM	N F Brannon	
Carrickfergus (Woodburn)	Site of abbey	M(N)	N F Brannon	*UJA* 1986
Deer Park Farms	Rath-mound	EC	C J Lynn	
Drumnakeel	Urn burials	BA	B B Williams	*UJA* 1985
Slievenacloy	Earthwork	PM	B B Wiliams	*UJA* 1985
Tievebulliagh	Industrial sites	Neo	J P Mallory (QUB)	
Co Armagh				
Armagh (McCrum's Court)	Urban	(N)	J A McDowell*	
Armagh (50–56 Scotch St)	Urban/ ecclesiastical	EC/M/PM	J A McDowell*	
Co Down				
Downpatrick (Demesne)	Standing stone	(N)	N F Brannon	*UJA* 1986
Newtownards (Court St)	Urban	M/PM	N F Brannon	
Kirkistown	Tower-house (SC)	(N)(C)	N F Brannon	
Co Fermanagh				
Glengesh	Portal tomb (site of)	?(N)	B B Williams	
Co Londonderry				
Coleraine (New Row)	Urban	EC/M/PM	N F Brannon	
Kiltierney	Burial mounds	IA	C Foley	
Tamnyrankin	Court tomb (SC)	Neo(C)	L N W Flanagan (UM)	

Site	Type	Period	Director	Published
Co Tyrone				
Dunmisk	Cemetery, enclosure	EC	R J Ivens*	
Tully	Mound	?	R J Ivens*	*UJA* 1985

1985

Site	Type	Period	Director	Published
Co Antrim				
Ballycraigy	Ring-ditch	BA	N F Brannon	
Craigs	Passage tomb (SC)	Neo	B B Williams	
Craigs	Field system	?M	B B Williams	
Deer Park Farms	Rath-mound	EC	C J Lynn	
Co Down				
Downpatrick (Cathedral Hill)	Ecclesiastical sites	EC/M	N F Brannon	
Downpatrick (The Grove)	Urban	M/PM	N F Brannon	
Co Londonderry				
Ballygroll	Round cairn	(N)	B B Williams	
Cuilbane	Stone circle		M J Yates	*UJA* 1985
Faughanvale	Occupation site	(N)	B B Williams	
Lissan, Tullynure	Enclosure	M	N F Brannon	
Maghera, Largantogher	Vicinity of early church	EC/M	N F Brannon	
Straid	Cist graves	BA	N F Brannon	
Co Tyrone				
Doras	Ecclesiastical enclosure	EC/M	J A McDowell*	
Dunmisk	Cemetery, enclosure	EC	R J Ivens*	

1986

Site	Type	Period	Director	Published
Co Antrim				
Ballyvaston	Occupation site	Neo/BA	B B Williams	
Connor	Ecclesiastical site	EC	N F Brannon	
Deer Park Farms	Rath-mound	EC	C J Lynn	
Glengormley	Rath	EC	N F Brannon	
Kells, Templemoyle	Priory	M(C)	N F Brannon	
Kilcoan More	Burials	M	B B Williams	
Co Armagh				
Armagh (48 Scotch St)	Urban/ ecclesiastical	EC/M/PM	J A McDowell*	
Killyfaddy, Dane's Cast	Linear earthwork	(N)	C J Lynn	
Co Down				
Downpatrick (Cathedral Hill)	Ecclesiastical sites	EC/M	N F Brannon	
Co Tyrone				
Dunmisk	Cemetery, enclosure	EC	R J Ivens*	

Year 19–		70	71	72	73	74	75	76	77	78	79	80	81	82	83	84	85	86	Totals
Antrim (80)	Rescue	2	5	6	6	6	4	5	5	4	4	2	1	1	3	8	4	5	71
	Research & SC												1	5		1	1	1	9
Armagh (24)	Rescue		2				2	3	2	2	2	1	1		2	2		1	20
	Research & SC	2												1				1	4
Down (34)	Rescue	1	1	1	1		1	1	1		1	2	2	3	4	2	2	1	24
	Research & SC	1	1	1				2	1		1			1	1	1			10
Fermanagh (14)	Rescue						2	1	3		1		1		3				11
	Research & SC				1	1					1								3
Londonderry (30)	Rescue				2	1	1		2		2	2		1	1	2	5		19
	Research & SC	2					2		2				1	3		1			11
Tyrone (29)	Rescue	2			1					1	4	4	5	3	1	2	2	1	26
	Research & SC											1		2					3
Yearly Total		10	9	8	11	8	12	11	15	11	16	11		20	19	20	13	10	211

Table showing number of DOE excavations carried out annually in each county, divided between rescue and research. The large number of excavations in Co Antrim reflects the pace of destruction of sites. Fermanagh, with only 11 rescue excavations, has lost fewer sites. SC = excavations on State care monuments in connection with conservation and presentation to the public.

94

Period	Site Type	70	71	72	73	74	75	76	77	78	79	80	81	82	83	84	85	86	Total Seasons by Site Type
Mesolithic					1	1	1												3
Neolithic	Settlement[1]	1	1													1	1	1	5
	Ritual[2]						1	2	2		4	2	2	1	1	2	4		21
Standing Stones							1								2	1			4
Bronze Age	Settlement	1			1									1			1		4
	Ritual[3]	1					2			1		2	1	2	1	2			12
Field Systems										1							1		2
Iron Age[4]		1							1						1	1		1	5
Early Christian	Settlement[5]	3	7	4	4	1	3	1	5	4	3	4	1	5	2	5	1	2	55
	Ecclesiastical[6]							2	2	3	2	1	2	3	2	3	4	1	25
Medieval	Settlement[7]	1				1	1			1	1	1	4		1		1		12
	Ecclesiastical	3			4	3	1			1	3	2	3	4	1	4	4		33
	Urban			3	2	2	3	6	3	3	3	1	2	1	1	2	1		33
Post-Medieval	Rural	1								1	1	1	2	3	1				10
	Urban						1	1	3	2	2	3	1	1	3	1	1	1	20

Table showing the types of sites on which excavations have taken place each year. If a site was important in two periods, both are tabulated. The excavations range in size from tiny evaluation exercises up to large projects.

1. Includes industrial sites 2. Graves and burial monuments 3. Includes cists, stone circles and burial monuments 4. Includes linear earthworks 5. Raths, cashels, crannogs, souterrains, house-sites, etc 6. Includes graves and inscribed stones 7. Castles, mottes and rural sites.

Appendix 2
ARCHAEOLOGICAL EXCAVATION AND THE LAW

All archaeologists who carry out excavations in Northern Ireland do so within the legislative framework of the *Historic Monuments Act (NI) 1971*, which, amongst many other subjects (such as monument protection), regulates excavation and the reporting of finds. One important section, which sets the Act apart from archaeological legislation elsewhere in the United Kingdom, contains the requirement that:

> '*A person shall not, save under and in accordance with a licence . . . dig or excavate in or under any land . . . for the purpose of searching generally for archaeological objects or of searching for, exposing or examining any particular structure or thing of archaeological interest*' (Historic Monuments Act (NI) 1971, pt IV, section 11 (1)).

This licensing restriction has many applications. Not the least valuable, and certainly the most frequently publicised, is its relevance to *treasure-hunting*, now a serious threat to the historic landscape. The use of metal-detectors has led to the destruction and looting of archaeological sites throughout the world, and to the rise of 'treasure-hunters' in Ireland and Britain. This section of the Act, in explicitly prohibiting excavation for archaeological purposes except with a licence, effectively makes the unlicensed treasure-hunting of antiquities illegal.

Central to the licensing system are the archaeological credentials of the person applying to excavate 'for archaeological purposes', and the nature of the proposed excavation. The Act is therefore a quality control designed to ensure that excavations are directed only by *bona fide* (though not necessarily professional) archaeologists, under research or rescue circumstances approved by the Government (in practice, the Department of Environment).

The issuing of a licence acts as a formal record that an excavation is to take place. The schedule of conditions attached to a licence includes the requirement that a summary report of the excavation results should be prepared with four weeks of work ending. This summary report provides interim answers to the main questions – where? when? why? what was found? A version is often published in the annual summary sections of various journals, to the benefit of fellow archaeologists and others, since the final report may take years to complete.

Except in rare cases (where a monument is in danger of damage or destruction and access negotiations have failed) the Historic Monuments Act requires that a licence should only be issued if the excavation takes place with the consent of the site's owner. Usually this requirement is easily met, and it provides an opportunity for the archaeologist and the landowner to discuss excavation logistics, health and safety responsibilities and the ownership of excavated material. Apart from Treasure Trove cases (where a coroner determines ownership) any excavated material legally belongs to the landowner. The archaeologist is usually keen to encourage the making over of the finds to a museum, where they can receive professional curation, be put on show for the public, or be available to researchers.

It should be remembered that, as with excavation licences, this consent-of-landowner constraint, and the common laws of ownership, apply to treasure-hunters.

Section 12 of the Historic Monuments Act obliges the finder of any archaeological object to report its discovery, and the circumstances of the discovery, to either the local police or the Director of the Ulster Museum. This report has to be made within fourteen days of the discovery, and the police or the Ulster Museum may hold any objects found for up to three months. This section has a particular application to antiquities – like cist burials, flint scatters, or coin hoards – accidentally discovered by members of the public. A prompt report often leads to a rapid inspection of the find-spot and the recovery of other finds or of information which can add greatly to the archaeological interest of the original finds. This provision in the Act was designed for such unexpected finds.

The large volume of finds from most archaeological excavations makes strict adherence to this reporting procedure unworkable in practice for the excavation director, but the controlled discovery techniques on an excavation mean that reporting is unnecessary.

Whatever the circumstances, whether on an excavation, a building site, a beach or in a graveyard, the discovery of precious metal objects brings the ancient law of Treasure Trove into action. Treasure Trove originated as a 'windfall' bullion resource for the medieval English Crown. If the original owner of a find of gold or silver could not recover it himself, the Crown benefitted. While the application of the law today stresses concern for the antiquarian rather than the monetary values of ancient objects, many archaeologists regret the archaic nature of Treasure Trove which is responsible for the exclusive concern with precious metal – gold and silver.

Anyone who finds an object wholly or partly made of precious metal is obliged to report the discovery to the police, who forward this report to the local coroner. Archaeologists directing excav-ations are not exempted from this procedure. An inquest is usually held, where, by a combination of statements by witnesses and specialists (a museum expert may formally identify the finds, for example), the coroner determines whether or not Treasure Trove applies. Only if the object is of precious metal, if it was hidden with the intention of recovery (however thwarted!), and if the rightful owner or heirs are not known, does the coroner declare the find to be Treasure Trove. The object is then formally seized by the Crown. If the finder acted properly in discovering and reporting the find he is normally rewarded with an *ex gratia* payment appropriate to its antiquarian value as was recently the case at Quoile Castle (*Fig 99*). If the object is not found to be Treasure Trove, ownership is generally regarded as resting with the owner of the land where the find was made.

The chance discovery of human remains naturally arouses great interest, and nobody would question the need for the police to be

100   Shoring in the excavation of an Early Christian period ditch.

99   Seven silver sixpences of Elizabeth I found in July 1986.

quickly informed. If ancient remains are suspected, rather than more recent foul play, an archaeologist is quickly on the scene. In cases of formal exhumation, as in the archaeological excavation of a graveyard, special permission has to be granted, but where ancient human remains are concerned a coroner's inquest may be held to satisfy any public concerns.

As in all walks of life, archaeologists and excavation staff are bound by Health and Safety regulations to ensure, as far as is reasonably practicable, the safety of their work-place (*Fig 100*). The potential hazards, including deep trenches, heavy machinery, underground cables, livestock and derelict buildings, mean that no excavation can operate without stringent safety precautions, and DOE(NI) archaeologists work within a code of practice.

GLOSSARY

BRONZE AGE

The beginning of the period is marked at around 2000 BC by the appearance of a new type of pottery, the Beaker, and by the occurrence in graves of small copper objects, like daggers, awls and flat axes. New burial rites, such as the single-grave cist, supplanted the megalithic tradition of collective burial and there was a rich variety of decorated pottery. Gradually bronze tools and weapons became more plentiful and these are represented by many stray finds and in discoveries of large hoards. Gold was used for the first time in making many types of dress ornament. Not every aspect of culture changed at the same time and it must be presumed that there was considerable continuity in craft practices with the later Neolithic.

CASHEL

A circular enclosure, comprising a wall, sometimes of great thickness, of dry-built boulders. Cashels usually occur in stony uplands or on coastal promontories and are thought to be the stone equivalent of earthwork raths.

CIST (CIST-GRAVE)

An underground cavity lined with stones on edge and covered with slabs, forming a stone 'box'. Short cists usually contain crouched inhumation burials or cremated bones with funerary pottery and date from the Bronze Age. Long cists, normally with extended inhumations facing east, date from the Early Christian Period.

CORBELS, CORBELLING

In the making of a corbelled roof each course of stones (called corbels) in the upper part of a dry-built wall projects inwards, beyond the course below. Eventually the walls come together so that the gap at the top can be closed with a single large stone. Corbelling is used in Neolithic court tomb galleries and the chambers of passage tombs.

CORDONED URN

A type of pot often found inverted over Bronze Age cremation burials, replacing food vessels. Related forms include encrusted urns and collared urns. There is a concentration of urn burials in north-east Ireland.

COURT TOMB

A type of Neolithic chambered tomb found in the north of Ireland and Scotland. The tomb comprises a rectangular or trapezoidal cairn containing a burial gallery of several chambers separated by jamb stones and roofed with large corbelled slabs. The gallery was entered from an open semicircular 'court', usually at the east end.

CRANNOG

An artificial island built of brushwood, timber, peat and sometimes soil and stones in a shallow lake or marsh and surrounded by a palisade or revetment of stakes and timber piles. A crannog usually supported several wicker or timber houses. Most crannogs were built as strongholds in the Early Christian period, but similar structures were built in the Late Bronze Age and crannogs continued to be built and used in the medieval period. They are difficult, but very rewarding, sites to excavate.

CROP-MARKS (or vegetation marks)

These sometimes appear on air photographs of ancient sites taken in dry weather. The presence of ditches is indicated by dark lines, resulting from greater moisture in the soil, and of buried walls or foundations by lighter, parched zones.

DENDROCHRONOLOGY

The technique of dating samples of oak wood, based on the fact that over a number of years the variable widths of trees' growth rings, each added annually to the outside, form characteristic patterns which do not repeat. The relative ring thickness is related to annual weather variations with the result that ring patterns are similar from tree to tree over large areas. A 'master chronology', extending backwards from the present, is built up by matching overlapping ring patterns from sample to sample. Each ring on the standard master chronology can be attributed to a particular year. When a suitable archaeological specimen is found its ring pattern (which must span at least 100 years) is compared with the master chronology. If an exact match is found at some point on the master, and if the bark is present on the specimen, the exact year and sometimes the season of its felling can be given. If the bark or sapwood is not present the date of the outermost ring is given to which must be added an unknown period for the felling and first use of the timber. Applications of the technique have been pioneered in the Palaeo-ecology Centre, Queen's University, Belfast.

EARLY CHRISTIAN PERIOD

A term applied in Ireland to the period from the establishment of Christianity in the 5th century to the coming of the Normans in the 1160s and 1170s. Art history, however, sometimes recognizes a Viking Age starting around 800, giving way to a Romanesque period at around 1050. The term 'Early Historic' is sometimes also used. Archaeologists' attempts to subdivide the period in terms of culture and settlement are hampered by poor dating evidence from excavations and the absence of pottery, apart from some early imports and the intractable souterrain wares of east Ulster.

FOOD VESSEL

A type of Early Bronze Age pottery normally found with burials in stone cists. Food vessels appear to have developed from Beaker pottery in southern Britain.

IRON AGE

This is the most obscure period in Irish prehistory even though it is the most recent. It is possible that horse-riding, wheeled transport and even Celtic language were introduced in the Iron Age. It is difficult to decide exactly when, some time after 600 BC, the ability to make iron tools and weapons became widespread. In the north of Ireland the Iron Age is certainly represented by stray finds of objects decorated in a distinctive curvilinear art style, called la Tène, after a site in Switzerland.

Burials of the period are rare and settlements virtually unknown. The only field monuments we have which are of Iron Age date are linear earthworks, probably made to mark or defend ancient boundaries or territories, and some ring-barrows. Most of the little evidence we have comes from the first two centuries BC and the first century AD. Apart from a few finds of imported Roman objects virtually nothing is known about the period from the second century to the fifth century AD, which remains an embarrassing and puzzling archaeological 'dark age' compared with the succeeding Early Christian period.

MEGALITHIC

Built of large stones. The term 'megalithic tomb' is applied to many forms of stone-built chambered tombs.

MESOLITHIC PERIOD

The Middle Stone Age, between the Palaeolithic (Old Stone Age) and Neolithic periods. The retreat of the ice-sheets northwards enabled people, still practising a Palaeolithic hunting and gathering way of life, to move northwards and to colonize Ireland for the first time before 6000 BC. The Mesolithic period is characterized by coastal shell middens and by flint implement forms such as large blades, microliths and flint axes. The period came to an end at around 4000 BC with the arrival of Neolithic techniques and settlers.

MILLEFIORI

A technique of decoration in which small multi-coloured patterned discs of glass were set in enamel on metalwork. This Roman technique was employed in Ireland in the Early Christian period.

MOTTE

A large, flat-topped conical mound with a continuous ditch around the base, built by the Anglo-Normans as a base for a timber castle or fortified house.

NEOLITHIC PERIOD

The New Stone Age which lasted from about 4000 BC to 2000 BC. Its beginning was marked by the introduction of agriculture, presumably by waves of settlers from Britain and Europe, with a consequent rapid increase in population, forest clearance, and an increasing pace of cultural change. Pottery was used for the first time, new forms of specialized flint tools appear and great numbers of polished stone axes, the most characteristic implement type of the period, have been found. Our earliest field monuments also date from the Neolithic period, for example megalithic tombs and hilltop settlements, such as the large enclosures on Lyles Hill (after which the most common pottery form is named) and Donegore Hill, both in south Antrim.

PASSAGE TOMB
A major type of later Neolithic megalithic tomb, often occurring in groups, in which a stone-lined passage leads to a burial chamber, roofed with large slabs or a corbelled vault. The outer edge of the mound is retained by a kerb of large stones. Stones of the kerb, passage and chamber may be decorated with pocked lines, normally forming motifs like spirals, chevrons and lozenges. Passage tombs are found along the Atlantic coasts of Europe from Iberia to Scandinavia and in Britain and Ireland. The most spectacular passage tombs in Ireland are in the Boyne Valley at Knowth, Newgrange and Dowth.

POST-HOLE
A term used for a small pit, the filling of which suggests that it was dug to hold an upright post. The post-hole contains packing, that is the soil and stones rammed in around the post, and the former position of the post may be indicated by a soft dark column of soil (sometimes called the 'post-pipe').

RADIOCARBON DATING
A complex and delicate laboratory dating technique carried out on samples of organically-derived carbon, usually charcoal or bone. All living things absorb small amounts of a radioactive carbon isotope, ^{14}C. On death the ^{14}C is no longer replaced and decays at a constant rate. By comparing the proportion of ^{14}C remaining with the amount which would have been in it when alive, we can reach an estimate of the time elapsed since the organism's death. Over the 40 years since the invention of the method, radiocarbon dating has made an enormous contribution to archaeology, particularly prehistory.

RATH
A small circular embanked enclosure, our most common type of field monument. A 'typical' rath would have a diameter of about 40 m, with an external ditch and a simple gap indicating the site of the entrance in the 1.5 m-high bank. Excavation has shown that raths were most commonly built as enclosed farmsteads in the Early Christian period,

but this form of small defended settlement may have originated in the Iron Age.

REVETMENT
A retaining wall or palisade at the edge of a dump of loose earth designed to maintain a steep face.

RING-BARROW
A low mound surrounded by a prominent ditch. These date from the Bronze Age or Iron Age. Often the mound covers a burial or burials, but in some examples burial may have taken place in the ditch.

RING-DITCH
A descriptive term applied to any ditch of circular plan, which, in the absence of further evidence, cannot be classified more closely.

SLOT
A long, narrow and relatively deep feature exposed in excavation. The use of the term is intepretative as it implies that the feature probably held upright timbers. If evidence for the woodwork survives in the fill the feature can be called a wall-slot or palisade-slot.

STAKE-HOLE
A vertical cylinder of soil, usually softer and darker than surrounding material, interpreted as the site of a driven stake which has rotted or been removed. While the hole may have been opened up with a probe before driving the stake, none of its fill is packing (unlike a post-hole).

SOUTERRAIN WARE
Coarse, hand-made, cooking pottery used in north-east Ireland in the Early Christian period (first recognized in early investigations of souterrains). The ware is typified by bucket-shaped vessels, some with grass impressions on the underside of the bases. Sometimes rims are decorated with finger marks or slashes and there may be applied or pinched-out cordons, plain or finger-impressed, below the rim. There are wide variations in the basic body and rim forms and in the fabrics. The origin of souterrain ware is unknown but it was the only local pottery used in Early Christian Ireland and it is very plentiful in some east Ulster raths.

SUBSOIL
Geologically-deposited and unaltered material, pre-dating human activity and, therefore, the level at which archaeological excavation stops.

TRIPARTITE BOWL
An Irish type of Early Bronze Age food vessel of bowl form with the profile divided into three distinct zones by horizontal ridges or carinations. They are sometimes decorated with lozenge or chevron patterns and are thought to have developed from Beaker pottery.

TUMULUS
A Latin word used by earlier students for any ancient mound believed to cover a burial or burials. The term is not in common use by archaeologists today.

VIKINGS
The people of Scandinavia who sailed south and west to Britain, Ireland and Atlantic Europe from the 9th to the 11th century, first as raiders, later as traders and settlers.

READING LIST

This selection offers suggestions for further reading of works of synthesis on the various periods, themes and methodology encountered in this book. Excavation reports and shorter articles appear in Irish archaeological journals, for Ulster the main journal being the *Ulster Journal of Archaeology*. The *Journal of the Royal Society of Antiquaries of Ireland* and the *Proceedings of the Royal Irish Academy*, section C are also valuable sources. In addition, there are many regional and county historical and archaeological journals.

P BARKER, *Techniques of archaeological excavation* (London, 1977).

G DANIEL, *The origins and growth of archaeology* (Harmondsworth, 1967).

E E EVANS, *Prehistoric and Early Christian Ireland: a guide* (London, 1966).

P HARBISON, *Guide to the national monuments in the Republic of Ireland* (Dublin, 1979).

HMSO, *An archaeological survey of County Down* (HMSO, 1966).

————— *Historic monuments of Northern Ireland* (HMSO, 1987).

M HERITY and G EOGAN, *Ireland in prehistory* (London, 1977).

H HODGES, *Artifacts* (London, 1971).

K HUGHES and A HAMLIN, *Celtic monasticism* (New York, 1981).

T E McNEILL, *Anglo-Norman Ulster: the history and archaeology of an Irish barony, 1177–1400* (Edinburgh, 1980).

F MITCHELL, *The Shell guide to reading the Irish landscape* (Dublin, 1986).

S P Ó RÍORDÁIN, *Antiquities of the Irish countryside* (revised edition by R de Valera, London, 1979).

M and L DE PAOR, *Early Christian Ireland* (London, 1978).

P RAHTZ (ed), *Rescue archaeology* (Harmondsworth, 1974).

INDEX

cist graves, xiii–xiv, 11–15, 29, 96, 99
Claudy, Londonderry, 12
clay moulds, 18, 20, 27, 40
climatic deterioration, 72
Cloghcor, Fermanagh, 90
cloisters, 52, 61, 72–5
Clough, Down, 48
Cloughorr, Antrim, 86
coins, xvii–xviii, xxi, 50, 56, 60, 64, 66, 72, 75, 77, 96–7
Coleraine, Londonderry, xxi, 1, 78–9, 89–90
Collins, A E P, vii, 7, 85–7
Connor, Antrim, 93
cooking pots, cast bronze, 75
Coolcran, Fermanagh, xx, 30–2, 91
conservation: xviii, 35, 52, 66, 84; excavations, xv, 29–30, 52, 66–9
convents, 58, 61
corbelling, 4, 99
corn-drying kiln, 55–6
Cornmarket, Belfast, 80
court tombs, xx, 3–8, 11, 99
Craigs, Antrim, 93
crannogs, 17–19, 99
Creggandevesky, Tyrone, xiv, xx, 3–5, 7, 89–91
'Crockgallows', Tyrone, 11–12
Crossnacreevy, Down, 86
crucibles, 18, 27, 34, 51, 60
crucks, 71
Cuilbane, Londonderry, 93
cultivation ridges, 37
curtain walls, 66–9

Dáire, 58
dam, masonry, 67–8
Daniells, M J, 87
daub, 18
Davies, Oliver, vii
de Courcy, John, 50, 64, 72, 75
de Croft, Gilbert, 72
Deerfin Lower, Antrim, 87
Deer Park Farms, Antrim, xv, xvii, xxi, 44–7, 92–3
Delaney, Tom, vii, 64, 86–8
dendrochronology, xv, xvii, xx, 23–4, 32, 99
Derry Churches, Down, 29
Derryloran, Tyrone, 91
de Sandal, Stephen, 72

destruction, vii, xiv, 17, 24, 41, 70, 96
Devenish, Fermanagh, xv, xxi, 52–4, 86–7
Devon, England, 65
diet, 27
ditches, xvi, xxi, 21, 39, 43–4, 47, 53–6, 62–3, 65–70, 76–7
Dobbin, William, 65
documentary sources, see written sources
Doddington, Sir Edward, 81–4
domestic ranges, 72–6
Domnach Mescáin, 29
Donegore, Antrim, 32
Doras, Tyrone, 91, 93
Dorsey, Armagh, xvii, xx, 21–4, 88
Down Cathedral, Downpatrick, 61
Downpatrick, Down, xxi, 50, 61–4, 92–3
drains, 33–4, 46, 74–6, 80, 83
Drumbroneth, Down, 89
Drumnakeel, Antrim, 91–2
Dublin, city, 66
Dunadry, Antrim, 72
Dúnchú, abbot, 55
Dungiven, Londonderry, xvi, xxi, 81–5, 87, 91–2
Dunmisk, Tyrone, xxi, 27–9, 93
Dunsilly, Antrim, 87

Early Christian period, xiii, xvii, xx–xxi, 8–11, 14–15, 27, 29–48, 51–2, 55–64, 72, 75, 97, 100
earthworks, 21–4, 44, 54, 57–8, 62–3; rectangular, 70–1
ecclesiastical sites, xxi, 27–30, 50–64
Emain Macha, Navan, Armagh, viii, 57
enamel, 26, 39
enclosures, 35–7, 39, 53, 58–9, 70–1; animal, 71; earthwork, 19, 70; monastic, 56; rectangular, xxi
England, 48
environmental evidence, xiii, xv, xviii, 2, 18–19, 21, 37, 47
Errigal Keerogue, Tyrone, 90
Evans, Estyn, viii
excavation: licences, vii, xix, 96; methods, xvi–xix

farm improvements, xix–xx, 3, 5, 11, 19, 23–4, 30, 32, 36–8, 41, 44
Farrell's Fort, Down, 85
Farrest, Tyrone, 90
Faughanvale, Londonderry, 93
Ferryquay Street, Coleraine, 78
fibulae, xx, 14, 26
fields, xxi, 36–37
field-walking, xiv, 1–2
finds, xvii–xviii, 17, 41, 66, 96–7; reporting, 96
Finkiltagh, Antrim, 86
fireplaces, see hearths
Flanagan, L N W, 88, 92
flint objects, xiv, 1–2, 5–6, 10–11, 18, 37, 51, 96
flint-working, xviii
floors, 51, 82–3
Foley, C, vii, 89–92
food vessels, 11, 100
forebuildings, 67
forecourts, 4, 6–8
Forensic Science Laboratory, Belfast, 69
foundations, 34, 48, 50–2, 65–7, 72–6, 80
France, 48, 50, 52–3, 64, 66
friaries, Franciscan, 57–8, 65, 72, 75–7

Gage, Mrs, 14
Gallanagh, Tyrone, 89
gate passages, 50
gates, 21
Germany, 53
'Giants Grave', 7
glass objects, post-medieval, 79
glass rods, 27, 60
glass-working, 27, 51
Glenarm, Antrim, 44, 75
Glengesh, Fermanagh, 92
Glengormley, Antrim, 93
Glenmakeeran, Antrim, 90
Gransha, Down, xxi, 38–41, 44, 86, 91
grave-covers, 50
grave-markers, 27, 50, 59
grave-mounds, 59
graves, see burials
graveyards, see cemeteries
Greencastle, Antrim, 88
Greencastle, Down, xxi, 66–9, 85–6, 88, 91
Greenisland, Antrim, 89

Printed in Northern Ireland for Her Majesty's Stationery Office
Dd.8869832 C.20 8/88 55–6136 3549

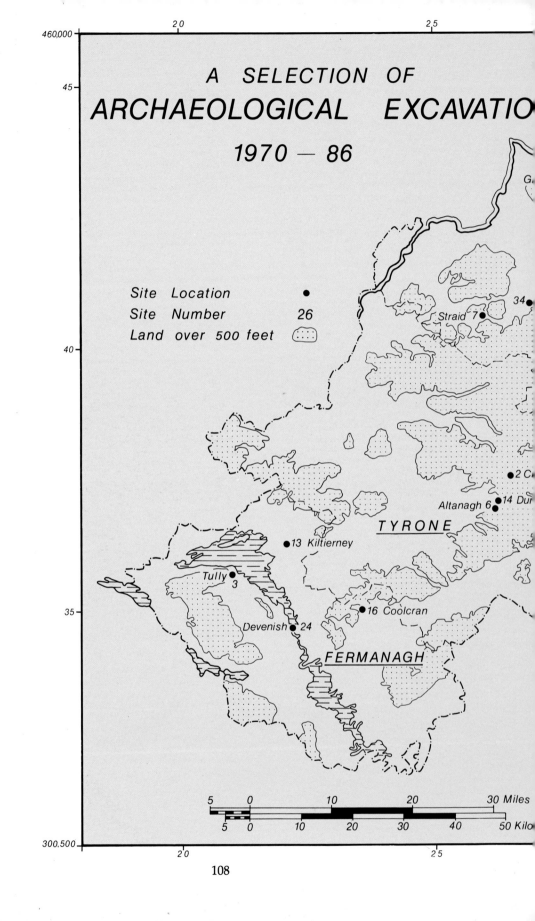

A SELECTION OF
ARCHAEOLOGICAL EXCAVATIO

1970 — 86

Site   Location   ●
Site   Number   26
Land   over 500 feet   ⠃⠃⠃

34 ●
Straid 7 ●

2 C

14 Dur
Altanagh 6 ●

TYRONE

13 Kiltierney ●

Tully ●
3

16 Coolcran ●

Devenish ● 24

FERMANAGH

5   0   10   20   30 Miles

5   0   10   20   30   40   50 Kilo

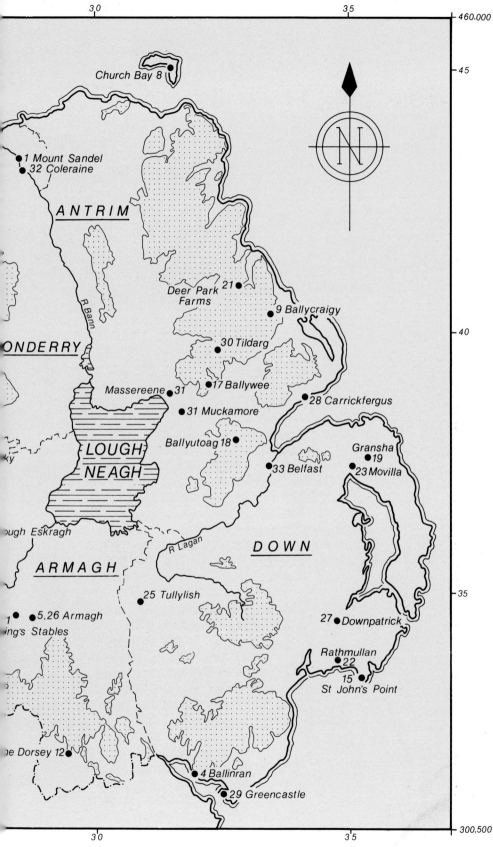